DOING BUSINESS
WITH SOUTH AFRICA

D1193451

DOING BUSINESS WITH SOUTH AFRICA

EDITORS

LES DE VILLIERS
JAN S. MARAIS
NIC. E. WIEHAHN

DE VILLIERS INCORPORATED

1981 De Villiers Incorporated
200 East 64th Street
New York, New York 10021

First edition 1981

Typesetting: Paul Middleton Advertising Pty. Ltd.
                 Johannesburg South Africa.

Printing: Tandem Press Inc.
                       New York.

CONTENTS

EDITORS

Les de Villiers, B.A. M.A. Former journalist, diplomat and senior government official. Regular contributor to leading journals and author of books on public affairs and business. Consultant on government and business relations. President of De Villiers Incorporated, New York and Johannesburg.

Jan S. Marais, B. Comm. (cum laude) D. Comm. (h.c.) Founder Trust Bank and recipient of several South African and foreign business awards. Member of Parliament and Chairman of marketing and industrial organisations. Director of companies, including De Villiers Incorporated.

Nic. E. Wiehahn, B.A. LL.B. LL.D. Supreme Court advocate, former member of Prime Minister's Economic Advisory Council and Chairman of Commission of Inquiry into Labour Legislation. (Wiehahn Commission). Former President of the Industrial Court of South Africa. Professor in Labour Law and Industrial Relations. Director of Companies and author of several books. Labour consultant.

INTRODUCTION

South Africa's political image as portrayed in many media is fearsome. Also many activist groups have made it their full time business to discourage others from doing business with South Africa.

Still, this did not prevent considerable overseas investment and trade with that country. South Africa today happens to be one of the world's twenty-six industrialized nations (the only one in Africa) and ranks fifteenth among trading nations.

This guide is not intended as a political analysis of present-day South Africa, but it will touch in brief on such issues where they directly affect international business. It would indeed be folly to presume that doing business with South Africa is like shopping and selling anywhere else in the world.

It is our aim to provide the business executive with a compact but complete guide to doing business with South Africa. We tried to keep this volume small enough to slip into the limited space usually available in the bulky briefcases of busy businessmen, without leaving any important questions unanswered.

The questions dealt with range from the momentous to the mundane. Such is the nature of foreign business. It does not only deal with issues such as investment incentives, royalties, and exchange control, but also advises on hotel facilities, restaurants, local customs, limousines, and the like.

In the preparation of this guide, we relied not only on many years of personal experience, but also drew on the expertise of others. If it assists more foreign entrepreneurs to find their way past the word barrier around a somewhat controversial country into its as yet largely untapped potential for business, it will have served its purpose.

At the same time we realise that a single volume such as this can hardly provide *all* the answers to *every* question. Consultancies such as De Villiers Incorporated will therefore continue to fill a need in assisting foreign individuals and corporations in doing business with South Africa.

De Villiers Incorporated is equipped to advise and assist foreign corporations in all areas relating to their business involvement in South Africa — both on an ongoing or *ad hoc* basis. In performing this task it relies in part on a panel of leading South African experts in the fields of labour, marketing, financing, politics, government, investment and trade.

De Villiers Incorporated
200 East 64 Street
New York, N.Y. 10021
Tel: 223-0306 935-0941

De Villiers Incorporated Pty. Ltd.
P.O. Box 4366
Johannesburg 2000
Tel: 41 0244/5

Chapter 1

PROFILE OF SOUTH AFRICA

LAND AND PEOPLE

The Republic of South Africa occupies 1.2 million sq.km. at the tip of the African Continent. It is five times the size of Britain, twice that of France and about one eighth the size of the United States.

Terrain

It consists of three basic types of terrain: (i) a narrow coastal belt with high rainfall in the east and desert conditions on the west coast; (ii) a series of escarpments stretching three hundred kilometres inland, varying in height between 1800 and 2100 metres, with peaks as high as 3300 metres; and (iii) an interior plateau averaging about 1200 metres above sea level.

Settlers

The Dutch first settled at what is today Cape Town in 1652, following in the wake of Portuguese discovery. Next came the French Huguenots as refugees from religious persecution in 1688. They in turn were followed by the British around 1820 after Britain took control of the fledgling Cape Colony. Also in smaller numbers came settlers from Germany, Sweden, and other parts of Europe.

During the 1830's the descendants of the Dutch and French trekked north to escape British rule. Already calling themselves Boere (farmers) or Afrikaners and speaking a language known as Afrikaans (derived from Dutch), these pioneers soon encountered adversity. Migrating from central Africa southwards at about the same time were several major black tribes, hungry for land and new conquests. They fought among themselves and against the Boere or Afrikaners.

Boer Republics

In the end the Afrikaners won. They established themselves in two so-called Boer Republics — the Transvaal and Orange Free State. The black tribes were allowed to retain the land which was in their possession as the hostilities ceased. Today these black homelands are a very important ingredient of the policy of *apartheid* or separate development. (See BLACK STATES POLICY).

This then was the position at the close of the nineteenth century. The Afrikaners in control of the Transvaal and Orange Free State, and Britain ruling the colonies of the Cape and Natal. The nine major black nations — varying from the Zulu to the Xhosa, Sotho, Tswana and Venda — in possession of so-called homeland areas scattered and fragmented along the eastern seaboard.

Fortune Seekers
Then diamonds and gold were discovered. Diamonds happened to be mostly in the Cape, but gold was Transvaal's alone. Thousands of fortune seekers and miners converged on this Afrikaner republic, mostly from the British Empire. Soon Britain was to use its voteless subjects who "suffered" at the hands of the Transvaal Boer government as a pretext to declare war and to wrest the riches for itself — or at least this is the way the Afrikaners explain the outbreak of the Anglo-Boer War at the close of the nineteenth century. Both Transvaal and Orange Free State lost their independence to Britain in this way.

Soon however, Britain under pressure of such notables as Winston Churchill granted full freedom to the Transvaal and Free State again in 1910 — not separately, but as part of the Union of South Africa, together with the former British colonies of the Cape and Natal. In 1961, South Africa became a Republic and withdrew from the British Commonwealth, but it still consists of four provinces: Transvaal, Orange Free State, Cape Province and Natal.

First?
Who was first? This is the question repeatedly raised in arguments about the rights of white and black in South Africa. The answer is simple: neither black nor white — but another group of people — the Hottentots and Bushmen.

Small in number, these nomads were on the shores when the first Dutch settlers arrived at the Cape. Today the Hottentots are extinct and the Bushmen only to be found in the desert regions of Botswana and Namibia, thousands of kilometres from Cape Town. But both their strains are to be found in the Coloured people, together with heavy traces of Malay and white parentage.

The Asian or Indian community never claimed to be first. They arrived in the 1860's as indentured labourers to work on the sugar cane fields of Natal. Most remained after their contracts expired.

Complex Make-up

This is the background in brief to South Africa's present day complex population make-up. The whites consist of about sixty percent predominantly Afrikaans speaking and forty percent predominantly English speaking South Africans. Most, however, speak both languages. The Coloureds mostly speak Afrikaans at home and are concentrated in the Cape, the Indians speak English and often one of their original native tongues and live for the most part in Natal; and the blacks belong to nine distinct nations living in different homelands and speaking different languages. In the white cities, however, a large so-called black urban population exists, speaking English apart from their own language and becoming increasingly Westernised in their ways.

Asians (Indians)	778 000
Blacks	16 214 000
Coloureds	2 494 000
Whites	4 408 000
Black Nations:	
Zulu	5 244 000
Tswana	1 364 000
Xhosa	3 040 000
North Sotho	2 037 000
South Sotho	1 686 000
Shangaan	788 000
Swazi	611 000
Venda	466 000
Ndebele and others	579 000
Foreign black workers	399 000

Source: Department of Statistics 1978.

GOVERNMENT AND LEGAL SYSTEM

On 31 May 1910 the Union of South Africa gained independence from Britain. It comprised four provinces — the former Boer republics of the Transvaal and Orange Free State and the former British colonies, Natal and the Cape. Each of these provinces retained a certain measure of authority in local matters through Provincial Councils, headed by an Executive Council and an Administrator.

Central government was modelled on the British Westminster system, comprising a House of Assembly and a Senate. Executive powers were in the hands of a Cabinet headed by a Prime Minister. A Governor General represented the British monarchy, signifying the link between South Africa and the British Commonwealth and performing mostly ceremonial tasks.

Republic

On 31 May 1961 South Africa withdrew from the British Commonwealth and became a Republic. The new Republic of South Africa retained basically the same form of government as before, but replaced the Governor General with a State President as Head of State. Executive power remained with the Prime Minister, as the leader of the majority party, and his Cabinet.

The South African Parliament, consisting of two houses, the House of Assembly and the Senate, continued to gather in Cape Town for its legislative sessions — lasting usually from end January until end June of each year. The members of the House were elected by Whites only, while Senators were chosen by all-white Provincial electoral colleges or nominated by the Government. Also this body happened to be open to white membership only until it was disbanded in 1980.

In compromise fashion when South Africa first gained its independence in 1910, Cape Town was declared the Legislative capital, while Pretoria, where the Executive spends six months of every year, became the Administrative capital. Bloemfontein was made the Judicial capital of newly independent South Africa and seats the Appelate Court, the country's highest judicial authority. This remained unchanged when South Africa became a republic in 1961.

Constitutional change

In 1980, with the elimination of the Senate, South Africa entered a new phase of constitutional change which is likely to continue deep into this decade. It was in essence the first step away from the old British Westminster system. Appointed to advise Parliament on constitutional changes, is the so-called President's Council, headed by a Vice-President and consisting of 60 appointees from South Africa's white, Coloured and Asian communities. This is seen by some as a first step towards active participation in central government for South Africa's Coloured and Asian minorities.

Black participation

As far as black participation in the decision-making process is concerned, the central White government still remains intent on granting such political rights in the traditional black homelands or states. Three of these black states have already opted for full independence and although they are not recognised by the United Nations as such, Transkei, Venda and Bophuthatswana are operating for all practical purposes as sovereign nations. Six others are earmarked for self-rule in the future. (See BLACK STATES POLICY). The end goal is some form of federalism or association between these independent black states and the remainder of South Africa — as mature and independent partners in much the same way as the Common Market. (See CONSTELLATION OF STATES).

Urban blacks

In the meantime, the ultimate role of South Africa's growing urban black population remains one of the country's most vexing problems. These Westernised and rapidly developing urban black communities in such major townships as SOWETO, Langa and Mamelodi, near "white" cities, have shed to a large extent their tribal ways and affiliations.

Legal System

South Africa's legal system is built on Roman-Dutch law. It originated in the Roman Empire and was used in the Netherlands until 1652 when the first Dutch settlers transplanted it to the southern tip of Africa.

In 1806 when the new Dutch colony in Africa was finally taken over by the British, they supplemented and modified the common law introduced by the Dutch. It was, however, mainly in statute law that the British influenced the South Africa legal system most.

Especially in the areas of mercantile, company and insolvency law many statutes are based on English law.

The highest court in the country is the Appellate Court, situated in Bloemfontein — the judicial capital of South Africa. There are seven provincial Supreme Court divisions, each presided over by a Judge President. Lower courts are called magistrates courts, serving so-called magisterial districts across the country.

BLACK STATES POLICY

Politics and economics interact. Sound business cannot be conducted without at least a basic understanding of the politics of any country. South Africa is no exception. Indeed, chances are strong that most foreigners long before they first discovered South Africa's business potential would have heard or read (even argued) about *apartheid.*

This term was first coined by the South African government in the late forties to describe its solution to difficult race problems. Today the same government prefers to talk in terms of *black states* or *separate development.* It had declared the word *apartheid* dead, but the policy itself is being modified gradually. So the debate abroad over the pros and cons of *apartheid* continues with the United Nations devoting more time and money and manpower to this issue than any other single matter.

The debate

Overseas *apartheid* is seen as oppression of black by white, while in South Africa, *the black states policy* is viewed as the only practical approach to a uniquely difficult racial problem. Through the past thirty years the fervour of the opposition to *apartheid* abroad has kept pace — and at times exceeded — the enthusiasm with which the policy was applied in South Africa itself. Many an unsuspecting businessman has found himself the target of activist groups who insist that doing business with South Africa is tantamount to financing oppression of blacks. (See DISINVESTMENT PRESSURES). It may strike such foreign businessmen as unusual that they do not encounter the same severe criticism when dealing with countries such as Russia, Red China and other such oppressive societies.

Still, discovering such inconsistencies in the anti-apartheid disinvestment crusade is unlikely to make the problem disappear. Every foreigner who intends striking up a lasting business relationship with South Africa needs to understand at least the rudimentary aspects of the *black states policy.* Not only would it assist him and his company in answering questions and criticism concerning investment in and trade with South Africa, it may also steer him towards a wealth of special incentives and concessions which form part and parcel of the black states concept. (See also DECENTRALISATION INCENTIVES and ESTABLISHING A FACTORY)

Essential philosophy

When white and black sorted themselves out in the largely uninhabited central and northern regions of South Africa in the mid-eighteenth century a number of so-called tribal homelands resulted. The blacks did not migrate from other parts of Africa in one single group but as several tribes or nations, fighting not only against the whites but among themselves. Eventually as peace was established these different black tribes or nations settled in their own separate parts of South Africa,

SO MANY MOUTHS . . .
. . . SO LITTLE FOOD

Every metre of available soil takes on a new importance. How to feed a constantly growing population from shrinking agricultural resources is the dilemma of the Eighties.
Triomf, South Africa's largest manufacturer and exporter of fertilisers is making their contribution by providing a worldwide solution.

PO Box 31755, Braamfontein 2017, Telex: 422249/422026 South Africa.

while the whites occupied the rest. (See also LAND AND PEOPLE).

Ever since, the claims of nations such as the Xhosa, Venda, Tswana, Sotho and others to these homelands have been recognised by successive South African governments. In the thirties the white government resolved to add land to these existing black states to make them more viable and since the early fifties active steps were taken to lead them to independence — separately.

At this stage three of these states have become independent — Transkei, Bophuthatswana and Venda. There are six more to follow. Eventually the white rulers hope that with all these national black states independent, pressures for one-man-one-vote in a united South Africa would cease.

Although the South African government puts great effort into making these homelands showcases and takes pride in favourable comparisons with other newly independent black countries, the programme has not been an unqualified success. Firstly, no one outside South Africa rushed to recognize these newly independent states of Transkei, Venda and Bophuthatswana — spawned as they were by *apartheid.* Secondly, even concentrated effort and assistance of all kinds could not stimulate enough economic growth in the homelands to stop the steady flow of black manpower away from the homelands into the white urban centres of Johannesburg, Port Elizabeth, Durban and so on.

The South African authorities insist that although a large number of black nationals work and reside in so-called white cities, this does not detract from the fact that these black states are truly independent. They point to Botswana, Swaziland and Lesotho, which were all three in effect homelands like the rest but given their independence by Britain, not South Africa. These three independencies in and around South Africa are generally poorer than the rest and have most of their men working in South African industries and mines anyway. Still, they are all recognised by the world and are fully-fledged members of the United Nations.

Stemming the tide

The argument in South Africa no longer concerns the validity of the *homelands* as such. Their existence has been accepted as a *fait accompli.* The main debate concerns the black tribesmen who left those black states and sprang roots in white South Africa — the so-called *urban blacks.* Although they are becoming increasingly important as an economic force both in buying power and the trade union movement, the urban blacks are still expected to exercise their political power in the respective homelands of their forefathers.

In the meantime the South African government is doing everything within its power to make economic conditions in the black states so attractive that it would stem the tide to the white cities. Under the aegis of such organizations as the Industrial Development Corporation (IDC) and the Corporation for Economic Development (CED), the South African government is offering a full range of unusually attractive tax and other incentives, to lure business and industry to these black national states. (See DECENTRALISATION INCENTIVES and ESTABLISHING A FACTORY)

Ultimate goal

Eventually the South African government envisages nine independent black national states willing to join with the remainder of the country as mature states in a regional economic and possibly defense pact. There is already a large measure of economic interaction and integration between these black states and the rest of South Africa. In fact, in recent times the South African government had actually given up on the idea of maintaining political boundaries as economic borders. It now talks about these political boundaries between the black states and the remaining part of the country as *soft borders* in an economic sense. Regional development programmes to spur on decentralisation no longer necessarily follow political planning in the finer detail.

Recently, also, the idea of establishing a sort of Southern African Common Market which would include not only these black homelands but other black states as well, was revived. The South Africans prefer to talk in terms of a Constellation of States.

(See also CONSTELLATION OF STATES and GOVERNMENT).

We mean way down to low interest rates in the lush, scenic green country of the growing Ciskei, which borders on the sunny and economically strong South Africa. This is the way Ciskeians talk big money : Loan capital at 2,8% plus building rental facilities at 5,8% of the cost of land and buildings, as well as attractive tax concessions.

Talk to the Ciskeian National Development Corporation - we'll advise you on a high return at a low level.

FOR A HIGH RETURN YOU HAVE TO GO LOW.

CISKEIAN NATIONAL DEVELOPMENT CORPORATION

Write to:
The Senior Development Manager
Ciskeian National Development Corporation
Private Bag X463
King William's Town 5600
South Africa
Telephone (0433) 21540
Telex 75-434 SA

CISKEI. AN INVENTIVE INVESTMENT

CONSTELLATION OF STATES

For many years successive South African governments have tried to accomplish some form of regional economic partnership in Southern Africa. Lately, with some of its own black homelands or national states already independent, the South African government has pushed once again for a specific regional arrangement encompassing itself and its black neighbours in a so-called CONSTELLATION OF STATES. (See also BLACK STATES POLICY).

The South African government considers the private sector as pivotal in this effort. Although governments can establish the framework for such co-operation, it is pointed out, real practical steps can only be implemented by the business sector. Obviously the business sector is not asked to perform charity. As they expand links, their profits naturally increase.

Catalyst

Past experience has shown that with its more advanced technology and larger economy, South Africa can serve as a catalyst for development elsewhere in the Southern African region. Cabora Bassa, Africa's largest hydro-electric project situated in Mocambique, could only be completed on the understanding that South African would purchase most of its power and contribute towards its actual construction. The harbour of Maputo, also in Mocambique, relies largely on excess freight diverted from South Africa, while the railways of this Marxist State happens to run with the help of South African technicians.

Proponents of the CONSTELLATION OF STATES idea like to cite the Mocambique example when sceptics insist that political differences between white-ruled South Africa and its black neighbours are too severe to allow for any formal economic partnership. There are, however, numerous other examples of co-operation between South Africa and independent black states diametrically opposed to this white-ruled country's internal race policies.

The Rand Monetary Area (a customs and monetary union) comprises South Africa and its independent black states — Transkei, Bophuthatswana and Venda — as well as Lesotho and Swaziland; the Southern Africa Regional Tourism Council (SARTOC) encompasses South Africa, Malawi and Swaziland; and the Southern African Regional Commission for the Conservation and Utilization of the Soil (SARCCUS) has seven members. Twelve individual labour agreements exist between South Africa and its neighbours.

Although it is evident that South Africa as the most developed and economically strongest country in the region, would continue to take the lead in providing labour opportunities, technological know-how, vaccines and the like, its government insists that it seeks no leadership role. The South African Prime Minister explained at a special gathering in Johannesburg of three hundred prominent business leaders that this proposed CONSTELLATION OF STATES does not imply a satellite relationship with South Africa at the centre of the solar system. Rather a grouping of states with common interests and developing mutual relationships.

Opportunities

Once this goal is attained it will obviously expand the scope also of foreign companies in South Africa. But business need not wait for formal agreements to be signed before they take advantage of the opportunities offered by the Southern African region. Many businessmen have discovered that even without formal agreements between governments in the Southern African region there is eagerness on the part of neighbouring states to do business with companies established and operating in South Africa.

LEVEL OF COMPETENCE

How competent is South Africa? How developed scientifically? How advanced technologically? How inventive?

These are questions bound to be asked by some abroad before they seriously entertain the thought of dealing with South Africa — given its rather isolated appearance on the southern tip of the so-called Dark Continent.

South Africa is selling technological know-how and scientific discoveries not only elsewhere in Africa but to the world's leading industrial nations.

Indicators

Here in brief are a few indicators by which to judge South Africa's level of competence:

★ It operates the world's only commercially viable oil-from-coal plants and is now marketing this process in countries such as the United States and Australia;

★ It developed its own unique uranium enrichment process — the only country outside the big powers to do so;

★ It performed the world's first heart transplant and subsequently developed the double-heart transplant technique, obviating removal of the diseased heart while implanting an extra one;

★ It operates the world's deepest mine, Western Deep Levels, at 11 800 feet below the surface;

★ It constructed the world's longest water tunnel diverting water from the giant Orange River to another river eighty kilometres away;

★ It designed the so-called Dolos breakwater block used extensively all over the world to protect shorelines;

★ It built at Richards Bay a phosphoric acid facility incorporating the world's biggest single-attack reactor;

★ It designed a new single chemical process for shrink and flame proofing of wool;

★ It has developed and is now marketing abroad a new fermentation process for the production of ethanol as a substitute for motor fuel;

★ It designed a new kind of ribbed plastic piping strong enough for use in sewer and drainage systems while using only forty percent of the material needed in normal plastic pipes — this ribbed piping replaces concrete and asbestos-cement pipes;

★ It built a narrow-gauge high stability railway bogie that has found ready markets in countries such as Australia, Japan and the United States;

SOUTHERN S

DURBAN
MALIBU
★★★T-YYY

CAPE TOWN
THE PRESIDENT
★★★★★T-YYY

JOHANNESBURG
SUNNYSIDE PARK HOTEL
★★★T-YYY ▣

PLETTENBERG BAY
BEACON ISLAND HO
★★★T-YYY

EASTERN TRANSVAAL
PINE LAKE INN
★★★T-YYY ▣

UMHLANGA ROCKS
BEVERLY HILLS
★★★★★T-YYY

BOPHUTHATSWANA
MMABATHO SUN

J
S
★

NATAL SOUTH COAST
THE BLUE MARLIN
★★T-YYY

KIMBERLEY
HOTEL KIMBE
★★★★T-YYY

BOPHUTHATSWANA
SUN CITY

PRETORIA
HOTEL BURGERSPARK
★★★★T-YYY ▣

SUN CITY
CABANAS

BLOEMFONTEIN
THE BLOEMFONTEIN
★★★★T-YYY ▣

JOHANNESBU
THE LANDDRO
★★★★★T-YY

JOHANNESBURG
THE RAND INTERNATIONAL
★★★★T-YYY

THE FINEST BUSINESS HO

Instant Reservations Head Office: Johannesburg 783-5333; London 580-6133; Frankfurt 06
Utell International Worldwide

UN HOTELS

CAPE TOWN
THE DE WAAL
★★★★T-YYY 📶

EASTERN TRANSVAAL
SABI RIVER BUNGALOWS
★★★T-YYY

MAURITIUS
SAINT GÉRAN

NNESBURG
HERN SUN'S AIRPORT HOTEL
T-YYY 📶

DURBAN
ELANGENI
★★★★T-YYY 📶

DURBAN
MAHARANI
★★★★★T-YYY 📶

PORT ELIZABETH
THE ELIZABETH
★★★★★T-YYY 📶

JOHANNESBURG
THE DEVONSHIRE
★★★T-YYY 📶

UMHLANGA ROCKS
CABANA BEACH
★★★T

UMHLANGA ROCKS
UMHLANGA ROCKS HOTEL
★★T-YYY

CAPE TOWN
THE NEWLANDS
★★★★T-YYY 📶

ZULULAND
ZULULAND SAFARI LODGE
★★★T-YYY

JOHANNESBURG
THE TOWERS
★★★★T-YYY

ELS IN SOUTHERN AFRICA.
/568; Los Angeles (213) 622-2506; Nationwide 800-421-8905; California only 800-252-0493.
contact your local travel agent.

★ It has developed several hybrid crops and new breeds of livestock as well as vaccines which not only increased its own productivity but also that of several neighbouring states;

★ It operates the largest coal-based ammonia plant in the world;

★ It has developed a mass algae culture method for producing protein-rich animal feeds from nitrogenous effluent;

★ It managed to supplement skimmed milk diets with an inexpensive protein, vitamin and minerals concentrate (PVM) and to develop three spray-dried products from Antarctic krill, providing new foodstuffs for itself and other parts of the world;

★ It succeeded in developing the world's first white enamel paint which does not discolour in diffused light;

★ It designed a high-pressure gas discharge laser which is now also in use elsewhere in the world.

These are some of the top-of-the-head responses of South Africans who were asked to name notable local accomplishments. There are un-doubtedly more discoveries and developments that could be included in a more complete resume.

R & D Spending

The U.N. Organisation for Economic Co-operation and Development devised a norm by which to quantify research and development spending in any country, namely, as a percentage of gross domestic product. In terms of this yardstick South Africa with 0.65 percent rates above Spain with 0.3 and below Canada with 1.00 and Belgium with 1.2 percent. At the top of the R & D totem pole are the United States (2.3 percent), West Germany (2.2) and Britain (2.1).

Half of all the spending on R & D in South Africa is by government and semi-government institutions, while business accounts for one-third and universities and non-profit organisations for the remainder.

Chapter 2

ECONOMIC PICTURE

ECONOMY

South Africa's gross national product totals U.S. $53 billion. This is about half that of Australia and one-fifth of Canada's GNP. Still, in Africa, South Africa's outstrips the rest in GNP and every other possible economic measurement. With only 6 percent of the African Continent's population it accounts for 55% of all the electricity generated and produces 85% of its steel.

While much of the rest of Africa starves, South Africa is a net exporter of food. Large quantities actually go to its black neighbouring states. It is also expected to become a net exporter of energy, despite its lack of oil. It already outstrips both France and Brazil in the production of energy — mostly from coal — and produces more crude steel than Sweden or East Germany.

Growth rate

After a recession in 1975, followed by moderate growth (1978: 2.5%; 1979: 3.75%), South Africa entered the eighties with a healthy growth rate of 7%. An upsurge in the gold price and export earnings generally, allowed the authorities to lower taxes, abolish compulsory loan levies on companies and individuals and to lift surcharges on imports. Instead of a deficit of $2 billion on its current account in 1976, South Africa finished the seventies and entered the eighties with a $3 billion surplus.

With exports grossing more than $20 billion and imports at $15 billion, South Africa managed a surplus on its balance of payments at the end of the seventies. Exports are headed by gold, base metals and minerals, diamonds, and prepared foodstuffs. Imports are mostly machinery and electrical equipment, transport equipment, and chemical and allied products. (See EXPORTS/IMPORTS).

Bet the Sheikhs wish this came out of the desert
(it will last longer than their oil)

. . . and South Africa has an abundance of it.

Almost anything that is derived from oil can also be obtained from coal. That is why, in 1971, long before the OPEC crises, AECI went back to coal to update the technology of extracting chemicals from coal.

This culminated in the world's largest nitrogen-from-coal complex, making explosives, fertilisers and urea. Also the gigantic Coalplex complex (another world's largest) that produces plastics, caustic soda and chlorine. These chemicals and their derived products are used in practically every industry and exported to world markets contributing to the security and resources of the western world.

Chemicals derived from coal: ammonia, blasting explosives, polyvinyl chloride (PVC), urea, limestone ammonium nitrate, ammonium nitrate, methanol, nitric acid.

AECI Limited Carlton Centre P.O. Box 1122 Johannesburg 2000 South Africa

International J16244

South Africa's gross domestic product relies mainly on manufacturing ($12 billion), mining ($9.5 billion), wholesale and retail trading ($6.5 billion), the financial sector ($6 billion) and farming and fishing ($4 billion).

Foreign participation played a vital role in South Africa's economic development in the past. One foreign expert claimed that British technology accounted for 40% of the growth of South Africa's GDP during the period between 1957 and 1972. South African economists themselves estimate that foreign capital is responsible for one third of the growth in that country's GDP. Continued foreign capital and know-how is generally considered as vital to the South African economy and actively sought and encouraged. (See FOREIGN INVESTMENT).

AGRICULTURE

Until the discovery of gold and diamonds in the late nineteenth century, agriculture was the backbone of the South African economy. Since then mining, and the manufacturing industry which followed in its wake, relegated agriculture to a lesser but still very important position. At the end of the nineteen-seventies agriculture accounted for 7 percent of South Africa's gross domestic product (GDP) and a third of its export revenues.

Exporting

South Africa is not only self-sufficient in food and agricultural products but one of the world's few net exporters. Its main exports are wool, sugar, maize, fruit and wine. Most of its wool clip goes to Japan and Europe, while its wines are sold to twenty-six countries including Britain, Canada, the United States, Europe and the Far East. Sugar is marketed mainly in Japan and Canada and fresh fruit (South Africa is the world's third largest exporter) to European countries. Maize — sold at a price in line with that of the Chicago Corn Exchange — is mostly sold to Japan, Taiwan and the United Kingdom.

Despite its self-sufficiency, South Africa obviously still has needs in the area of agriculture. Coffee, rice and tea were major import items in recent years. Following are the export/import figures for the late seventies:

Exports	1975	1976 R-million	1977
Total products (excluding gold bullion)	3 983,2	4 532,1	5 863,2
Total agricultural products (unprocessed)	642,1	586,6	611,3
Total agricultural products (processed)	606,9	650,8	726,2
Wool	116,8	173,7	190,7
Mohair	18,1	24,7	23,9
Karakul pelts	17,3	26,0	41,4
Hides and skins	25,8	47,1	49,7
Maize and maize products	302,5	236,5	190,0
Preserved fruit and jam	103,9	131,8	126,1
Sugar	282,3	209,8	233,4
Citrus fruit	110,1	64,2	94,2
Deciduous fruit and table grapes	59,3	82,7	56,1
Groundnuts and groundnut oil	25,4	12,5	17,4
Imports			
Rice	26,0	26,8	30,9
Coffee	14,6	23,9	50,6
Cocoa beans	9,0	7,5	6,8
Rubber (unprocessed)	16,4	28,0	28,4
Tea	19,7	22,9	36,1

Conditions

The volume and sophistication of the South African agricultural industry may give outsiders the mistaken impression that this country is ideally suited for crops and livestock. It is, in fact, mostly arid and unsuitable and it is only through sustained experimentation and adaptation that agriculture expanded the way it did.

South Africa has developed its own breed of cattle and sheep, new feeds, hybrid crops and new fruit and vegetable varieties to cope with droughts. It developed its own weed and pest control methods and even supplies other African territories with millions of vaccine doses per year to combat local animal and plant diseases. It was the first country to enact and enforce quality controls for agricultural exports.

In view of these developments it is evident why the agricultural attachés stationed at some of South Africa's major Embassies abroad, are in a position to exchange useful information.

Irrigation

Since the early nineteen-sixties South Africa has actively engaged in the construction of several irrigation dams to assist semi-desert areas in becoming crop-oriented. The largest is the Orange River Project, started in 1962 and still under construction. It is a thirty year development which will affect most of the interior of South Africa by way of irrigation and hydro-electric power. One of its stages involved the construction of the world's longest continuous water tunnel carrying water underground from the Orange to the Fish River, eighty kilometres away.

Mechanization

Tractors are still mostly imported. Sixteen different makes of mainly the 53 to 60 kW power class are marketed. The local farming machinery industry, however, supplies in all the needs as far as tillage equipment and other power machines are concerned. It is evident though that room for new equipment and forms of mechanization will continue to exist. The size of the market can perhaps best be judged from the fact that slightly more than a million people are employed on some 75 000 farming units.

Subsidies

As in other developed countries the government maintains a system of subsidies to ensure stability in prices. Although the Department of Agriculture oversees the industry officially, anyone who intends to market machinery or patented products to the farming community should best address themselves to the South African Agricultural Union and some three hundred individual farmer's co-operatives. Promotion of implements, incidentally, is largely done by way of agricultural shows of which there are literally tens per year. The largest single event happens to be the Rand Easter Show in Johannesburg, taking place as the name indicates, during Easter every year.

Homelands

In contrast to the sophistication of the farming industry in South Africa, agriculture in the black homelands is mostly on an underdeveloped subsistence basis. In its efforts to stimulate growth in these national states, the South African government gives high priority to agriculture. Entrepreneurs who wish to establish processing plants relying on farming produce will find the authorities most helpful and the incentives outstanding. (See also BLACK STATES POLICY and DECENTRALISATION INCENTIVES)

MINERALS

Minerals account directly and indirectly for over a quarter of South Africa's Gross Domestic Product and in the region of 70 percent of its export revenue. It was the discovery of gold and diamonds at the turn of the century that heralded South Africa into the Twentieth Century as an industrial society. Since then mining of some fifty minerals has encouraged large scale investment, immigration and trade from abroad — and the growth of that country into one of the world's industrialised nations, the only one in Africa.

Golden Beginning

Some still maintain that South Africa is basically the country of gold. This view is perpetuated by millions of happy Krugerrand buyers who acquire these gold pieces as a hedge against inflation. Gold, it is true, enabled South Africa in recent times to prosper while economies elsewhere in the developed world sagged under OPEC oil price pressures and high inflation. In one single year — 1979 — the rise in gold price and production accounted for an increase in profits for South Africa of 70.6 percent. The following year it envisaged a growth rate in its economy of at least 7 percent and summarily lowered taxes across the board — while most others struggled to balance budgets and to control inflation with recessionary methods.

World Ratings

South Africa's mineral story is, however, hardly one of gold alone. In terms of overall mineral output this country ranks third in the Western World after the United States and Canada. As a source of strategic minerals it is the Free World's most important supplier. Western strategists note with some measure of alarm that as a result of a geographical freak South Africa and Russia contain between the two of them most of the world's vital and strategic minerals — a fact that has obviously not escaped the notice of the Soviet authorities either.

Russia happens to use most of its own production in these strategic minerals — and even if it didn't it would probably be reluctant to sell to the Western world other than at inflated prices. So South Africa remains the only real source for the Western world as far as minerals such as chrome ore, platinum, manganese, and vanadium are concerned. Without for instance manganese or chrome the wheels of industry will come to a halt as both these elements are needed in the manufacture of high quality steel. Some experts maintain that a cut-off in either would be more devastating to the Western world than a complete embargo in oil.

This is how South Africa rates on the Western world's minerals chart:

SOUTH AFRICA'S ROLE IN WESTERN WORLD MINERAL SUPPLY, 1978

MINERAL COMMODITY	EXPORTS RANK	±%	PRODUCTION RANK	±%	RESERVES RANK	±%
Platinum group metals	1	91	1	91	1	89
Vermiculite (crude)	1	80	2	38	2	29
Vanadium (metal)	1	73	1	56	1	90
Gold (metal)	1	67	1	73	1	64
Manganese metal	1	67	1	55	-	-
Ferrochrome	1	58	1	33	-	-
Andalusite/Sillimanite	1	49	1	37	1	45
Diamonds (gem)	1	46	1	46	1	large
Chrome ore	1	40	1	51	1	84
Manganese ore	1	36	1	36	1	93
Ferromanganese	1	22	2	12	-	-
Fluorspar	2	21	1	13	1	46
Uranium (metal)	2	20	3	11	2	18
Zirconium (concentrate)	2	9	3	11	3	12
Titanium (ilmenite, rutile)	3	20	3	18	5	8
Asbestos (fibre)	3	12	3	10	2	8
Coal (bituminous, anthracite)	4	13	4	7	4	10
Antimony (metal)	6	7	2	20	2	18
Iron ore	7	5	7	5	6	6
Nickel (metal)	7	3	5	5	5	8
Copper (metal)	7	3	8	3	13	2
Tin (metal)	9	1	8	2	13	1

(Source: S.A. Minerals Bureau)

Mining Industry

There are more than 900 mines and quarries in operation in South Africa, including the world's richest, largest and deepest. Its minerals industry is one of the most highly sophisticated and in recent years South Africa has become an exporter not only of minerals but of technology and mining machinery. Its mines employ 700 000, many of whom are contract workers from neighbouring African states.

Production and Exports

Some 50 minerals mined in South Africa account for a total annual sales figure of around R15 billion. Of these 43 are mineral commodities exported to more than 90 countries located mainly in Western Europe, the Far East and North America. The total revenue from exports in 1979, excluding ferro-alloys and mineral manufactures such as phosphoric acid, amounted to R8,5 billion.

Gold's Future

In the seventies South Africa experienced a boom in base minerals, greatly helped by downstream processing of ferro-alloys and phosphoric acid; impressive strides in coal and iron ore utilisation, both in export and locally; and first a near-collapse of the gold price, followed by a dramatic recovery at the end of the decade.

During these years gold contributed on an average — despite fluctuations in price — 58 percent of South Africa's total revenue from mineral sales abroad, while the rest accounted for 42 percent. The experts predict that gold production will decline in volume during the eighties as even the low-grade ores become scarcer — but they expect that an increase in the price will keep the revenue growing at a steady pace — enabling gold to remain more than half of South Africa's total mineral revenue abroad.

Following is a projection by South Africa's Minerals Bureau based on reasonably conservative gold price increases:

YEAR	1980	1981	1982	1983	1984	1985
Output (tons)	685	692	692	688	682	676
Price ($/oz)	450	506	569	640	720	810
Revenue (R billion)	7,8	8,9	10,1	11,3	12,7	14,2

Average exchange rate US$ to Rand = 1,25
(Source: S.A. Minerals Bureau)

Energy Minerals

In view of the growing demand for cheaper energy in the wake of OPEC's price hikes, South Africa's coal and uranium supplies are assuming greater importance. Apart from providing almost 90 percent of South Africa's electricity output, coal is extensively used in gasification or synfuel programmes and for the production of metallurgical coals and formed coke. It also gave birth to a large chemical industry. (See ENERGY and MANUFACTURING INDUSTRY).

At the end of the seventies South Africa started developing a large export programme for coal to mostly Europe and North America. It is not the world's largest source of coal — ranking fourth in the Western world at present — but it delivers at very competitive prices. Total exports in 1979 amounted to R600 million, with South Africa selling large quantities to the United States — a country described by some as the Saudi Arabia of coal!

Uranium in South Africa is essentially a by-product of gold mining. During the mid-seventies these mines almost doubled their production of uranium in anticipation of an increasing demand for this material. When it did not materialise, they simply switched their emphasis to gold again. In the expected growth of nuclear power stations during the eighties, the uranium factor will once again become important.

The Scope

In view of the sophistication of the South African mining industry foreign investors may well decide that there is very little scope left for direct participation in mining ventures in that country. Yet, overseas corporations still continue to find room for expansion into South Africa, either in joint ventures with local companies or in consortium with overseas partners. In the illustrious history of South African mining overseas participation has always been crucial — President Herbert Hoover, incidentally, before he became President of the United States, was a mining engineer in Johannesburg.

For those who depend on minerals for their livelihood and profits — either as middlemen or manufacturers — South Africa is a likely source, if not the only one. Individuals and corporations also have scored handsomely in buying and selling South African mining shares. (See JOHANNESBURG STOCK EXCHANGE)

Prospecting

Prospective prospectors need to apply to the South African Government if they wish to search for natural oil or precious metals. In the case of base metals they need the permission of the owner of the land. Before they set out to do so, they should realise that in a sophisticated mining country such as South Africa the possibility of discovering ones eldorado in this manner is slim in view of the alertness of many well-heeled and organised mining houses.

More information can be obtained from:

The Secretary of Mines
Private Bag 59
Pretoria 0001

Quest for Oil

South Africa has every imaginable important mineral in abundance — except bauxite and oil. The South Africans seem to be unconcerned about the first because they can get it in abundance from elsewhere, but oil, in view of its strategic value, bothers them. The authorities, obviously reluctant to believe that South Africa has no worthwhile oil resources established SOEKOR (Southern Oil Exploration Corporation) in the mid-sixties to undertake, encourage and co-ordinate with private companies an intensive search for oil. Exploration has been done since on land and off-shore with minor strikes registered on land and a major find of natural gas off-shore. They are still trying and welcoming overseas involvement.

Two Way Street

Whereas mining development in South Africa in the beginning relied heavily on overseas expertise and capital, the reverse is happening to-day. In every part of the world where mining is important South African expertise and equipment are utilised in one way or another. The greatest single foreign investor in the United States — almost exclusively in mining — is South Africa's Anglo American Corporation, which together with six other major companies dominates the mining scene on its own turf as well.

Statistical Data

For accurate and reliable statistical data about mining in South Africa, the following source is recommended:

Minerals Bureau
Private Bag 4
Braamfontein 2017

Telephone: Johannesburg 725 3360
Telegraphic: MINBURO

Useful publications and reports about mining in South Africa are available from:

Public Relations Department
Chamber of Mines of South Africa
P.O. Box 809
Johannesburg 2000.

MANUFACTURING INDUSTRY

At the end of the nineteenth century the discovery of gold and diamonds transformed the face of South Africa. Mining was the first stimulus for the development of a manufacturing industry. (See MINERALS). Two world wars further accelerated the process and today South Africa is rated by the United Nations Organisation as one of the world's twenty-six industrialised nations — the only one in Africa.

Main activity

As a major producer and exporter of agricultural products, it is logical that much of South Africa's manufacturing industry would centre around this sector. The processing of foodstuffs and wool, together with mineral-related manufacturing plants occupy centre stage. (See AGRICULTURE).

In its efforts to become more self-sufficient in the area of energy, despite a lack of oil resources, South Africa built several oil-from-coal plants. (See ENERGY). These SASOL installations in turn, as with normal oil refineries, provided the basis for a thriving chemicals industry. In fertilizer, for example, South Africa has become one of the world's major producers and exporters. Also coal-based in South Africa is the world's largest ammonia plant, PVC complex, and only modern methanol plant.

Scope

Despite its relatively high level of industrialisation, South Africa is still dependent on the outside world for much of its manufactured goods. This presents the prospective exporter from abroad sufficient scope for trade — and more importantly, provides foreigners who wish to establish factories in South Africa, with special opportunities. In its endeavours to replace imported capital goods with local manufactures, the authorities offer a wide range of incentives to new industries. (See ESTABLISHING A FACTORY and EXPORTS/IMPORTS).

The following table provides an overview of the manufacturing industry at the close of the seventies:

	Number of establish-ments 1976	1) Production 1977 (R-million)	Imports 1977 (R-million)	Exports 1977 (R-million)	Total employ-ment 1977
Processed foodstuffs	1 925	3 148	138	629	161 400
Beverages and tobacco	328	1 451	36	14	29 600
Textiles	606	1 049	259	110	109 500
Clothing	1 212	586	27	19	94 100
Footwear	136	187	21	4	17 000
Wood and wood products	711	259	31	22	52 000
Furniture	788	331	7	1	24 500
Paper and paper products	193	743	127	110	34 800
Printing and publishing and allied industries	1 144	376	35	3	34 600
Leather and leather products	156	98	17	14	9 200
Rubber products	77	314	39	12	17 200
Basic industrial chemicals	188	1 195	490	197	
Other chemicals	519	2 669	211	145	78 700
Plastic products n.e.i.	346	291			19 200
Mineral products (non-metallic)	1 071	739	61	39	85 500
Iron and steel basic industries	137	1 949	95		
Non-ferrous metal basic industries	97	407	60	1 283	105 500
Metal products	2 377	1 449	147	47	118 700
Machinery (excluding electrical)	1 091	1 321	1 299	178	76 500
Electrical machinery and equipment	589	1 027	520	41	59 600
Motor vehicles	685	1 227	615	52	
Transport equipment	154	422	300	33	86 800
Professional equipment	130	42	187	14	5 900
Other manufacturing industries	692	312	77	213	22 100
TOTAL	15 352	21 593	4 801	3 180	342 400

1. Estimated by the value of sales
Source: South African Statistics 1978

State participation

Only in fields where the private sector found itself either unwilling or unable to develop industry, the South African government became involved. As early as 1928 the Iron and Steel Corporation was developed by the state to supply allied industries. Today ISCOR has three plants — at Pretoria, Vanderbijlpark and Newcastle in Natal — and exports through Saldanha iron ore to Japan and the world.

The S.A. Coal and Gas Corporation (SASOL), another state undertaking, operates the world's only oil-from-coal plants. SASOL I and II are already in operation and III is scheduled to be on stream in the mid-eighties.

African Metals Corporation (AMCOR) was established to produce pig-iron, ferro-alloys and dolomite, as well as rock phosphate and high carbon chrome. The Phosphate Development Corporation (FOSKOR), another state undertaking, produces phosphate concentrates and supplies private fertilizer manufacturers. ALUSAF was created to make South Africa self-sufficient in primary aluminium metal needs.

At the core of the South African government's participation in the manufacturing field, is the Industrial Development Corporation (IDC). Established during the Second World War, this state corporation assists and supplements private enterprise — often by extending financing, and sometimes by getting involved itself in establishing operations. Its list of successful sorties in the private sector includes such present-day giants as the following which were all assisted or sponsored in one way or another; SASOL, SAPPI (S.A. Paper and Pulp Industries), SAFMARINE (S.A. Marine Corporation), FOSKOR, SOEKOR (Southern Oil Exploration Corporation), SAICCOR (S.A. Industrial Cellulose Corporation), ALUSAF and SACC (S.A. Cable Company).

Still, the authorities insist that it has never been and will never be its intention to compete with the private sector. In fact in a few instances, such as Klipfontein Organic Products it sold the operation after it became profitable and more recently in the case of SASOL it allowed for public shareholding. (In this instance, incidentally, the share issue to institutional investors was quickly filled and the one available to individual investors oversubscribed thirty-one times).

Government through the IDC continues to involve itself where private business shows reluctance — as long as there is a specific need or strategic importance attached to a venture. At the same time the IDC is, together with the Corporation for Economic Development (CED), involved in encouraging and assisting industrial development in and around the so-called black national states). (See BLACK STATES POLICY, DECENTRALISATION INCENTIVES and ESTABLISHING A FACTORY).

FISHING INDUSTRY

South Africa is not a major exporter of fish. During the seventies its world ranking in terms of volume of fish caught actually declined from seventh to fifteenth.

Around its 3 500 kilometres coastline South Africa has a full range of sea creatures including endless types of fish, octopus, mussels, oysters and other shellfish. The Sea Fisheries Branch of its Department of Industries keeps a watchful eye on the South African fishing zone covering a two hundred nautical mile band around its coast.

Despite its membership of the International Whaling Commission, South Africa has long ceased to catch whales. Sealing is done under strictly controlled circumstances, while tuna catching is left to recreational fishermen — and increasingly, long-range foreign ships.

Rock lobster

It is by its rock lobster that South Africa is known in good restaurants around the world.

Strict conservation, tight quotas, severely enforced size requirements, and limited catching seasons keep South African lobster in short supply abroad — even though eighty percent of the total yearly catch of some ten thousand tons is exported. Marketing is handled by the South African Frozen Rock Lobster Packers, which mostly sells frozen tails and cooked products, and the Cape Rock Lobster Exporters Association which deals in whole lobster. Main markets are the United States, Europe and Japan.

WINES

South African wines are backed by a long history and rich tradition, that stretches back as far as the first settlement at the Cape. Jan van Riebeeck, first governor of the Cape, and founder of the settlement, planted the first vines in 1655 from European rootstock. An entry in his diary on 2nd February 1659 reads: "Today, praised by the Lord, wine was made for the first time from Cape grapes."

Viticulture at the Cape was greatly stimulated with the coming of the French Huguenots in the latter part of the eighteenth century. They brought with them the skills and expertise, and a love for wine. Since those days the quality of Cape wines has increased steadily. Modern technological advances in the field of viticulture and wine-growing and the skills of highly qualified cellar technicians today complement the ideal climate of the Cape and the noble cultivars used for wine-making to produce wines that compare with the finest produced elsewhere.

The South African wine-growing areas are situated at the South and South-western tip of the Continent in a radius of about 300km from Cape Town. It enjoys a perfect Mediterranean climate and its soil types favour the growing of the vine. Wine-growing is the oldest and most important stable agricultural pursuit and at the base of the economy of the area.

White Wines

The white wines of the Cape have found favour with many consumers the world over. The most extensively planted white cultivar is Steen, also known by its French name, Chenin Blanc. From it wines are produced that compare most favourably with some of the white wines of Germany and France. These are fresh, fruity wines with particular style and character that derives from the Cape's soil and climate.

Fine white wines are produced also from cultivars such as Riesling, Clairette Blanche, Colombard, Sauvignon Blanc, Muscat d'Alexandrie and lately, from new plantings of varieties such as Gewürztraminer, Buckettraube and Kerner.

Although the Cape climate may seem to favour the production of fuller-bodied wines, these white wines, made by a process of cold fermentation, are delicate and fruity with an attractive flowery bouquet.

Red Wines

The Cape reds have equally pleased discriminating palates in many parts of the world. They are made from noble European cultivars such as Cabernet Sauvignon, Shiraz, Pinot Noir and Cinsaut which are sometimes blended to produce wines of great interest and unsurpassed quality. A uniquely South African variety — Pinotage — which is a hybrid of Pinot Noir and Hermitage, is used to produce a fruity, full wine with a character all of its own.

The Cape climate is, of course, ideal for the production of great aperitif and dessert wines. Sherry wines from European varieties such as Palomino, and made in the classic fashion by fermentation under "flor," have won acclaim in many countries, so have the port and the sweet muscat dessert wines.

Cape brandies have also been recognised for their high quality for many years. They are produced from the classic European grape varieties in areas particularly suited to their growth, in pot-stills and matured in oak under the most stringent Government control in the world.

Origin Seal

Realising the importance played by nature (the soil, climate and location) in determining the character and quality of a wine, South Africa's Wine of Origin legislation has provided for the demarcation of wine-producing areas which may range from an estate to an entire region; it also covers the use of cultivar names and the vintage.

Along with the art and skill of the winemaker, the origin seal which guarantees the contents of the bottle, encourages the production of wines with individual character — as different as the areas in which they are produced and the cultivars used.

Exports

Although the wines and brandies of the Cape are mainly consumed in the Republic, they have, for many years, been marketed successfully overseas. These exports emanate mainly from the KWV which markets Cape wines and brandies in some 30 countries across the globe.

KWV is the Afrikaans abbreviation for "Co-operative Wine Growers' Association". It is the central controlling body of the wine industry at producer level and all wine-growers (some 6 000) are members. The head-office is in Paarl, in the heart of the South African wine country. From its cellars are exported 80% of all Cape wines that are shipped abroad. One of its most important tasks is continuously to regulate and control quality and by using the best known cellar techniques and most highly qualified wine experts to ensure that only wines which satisfy the highest quality standards are sold under its label overseas. It operates one of the largest and most modern cellar complexes in the world from Paarl, with other cellars and distilleries spread throughout the wine-producing regions.

During the last half of the '70s KWV wines showed phenomenal growth in overseas markets and present sales indicate that this upsurge should continue in the '80s. South Africa has, for instance, now moved up to a secure fifth position of those wine-producing countries exporting quality red and white light wines in bottle to the United Kingdom. Shipments in bottle from the Cape are only exceeded by those from the traditional wine-producing countries of France, Germany, Italy and Spain.

The growth in volume can directly be related to the quality image these wines have achieved. They are now recognised as wines of excellent quality, comparable with the best European wines in their price range. And good value for money is easily recognised by the consumer overseas.

Character

KWV wines have often been praised by experts abroad as being clear and brilliant, fruity and true to character and with the ability to travel well. There has also been favourable comment on the low sulphur values of the wines — extremely low when compared with products from other countries.

The strongest growing export market is most definitely the United Kingdom but in Europe sales have been increasing in West Germany, and the Benelux countries, among others. Canada is also regarded one of South Africa's most prominent wine markets and the KWV brand-name PAARL has long been well-established in the mind of the Canadian wine-lover and brandy connoisseur.

It is now generally acknowledged in most parts of the world that a bottle of Cape wine can be served with pride for enjoyment by the most discriminating palates.

QUALITY CONTROL

In South Africa manufacturers can submit their products to severe testing (almost abuse) at the *South African Bureau of Standards* — a government-subsidised research organisation with impeccable credentials for impartiality and honesty.

With close to sixty laboratories and more than a thousand scientists, technicians, and other personnel at its disposal, the SABS is equipped to test almost anything from a needle and thread to giant transformers and freight containers.

Should these products comply to the rigid standards set by the SABS they become entitled to display the Bureau's special seal of quality. This SABS seal has become a familiar first requirement on the part of discriminate buyers in South Africa and even abroad where South African products are sold. At latest count there were one thousand two hundred permit holders marketing 1 600 brand name products under the SABS seal.

Sometimes the Bureau of Standards is requested by purchasers to test consignments against specifications before delivery — ensuring in this manner that they get exactly what they are paying for.

Obviously foreign businessmen who intend to manufacture their product in South Africa — as well as those who wish to export already fabricated goods to that country — are well advised to apply at the SABS for quality tests and certification.

Further information can be obtained from the SABS itself at the following address:

South African Bureau of Standards
Private Bag X191
Pretoria 0001.

Chapter 3

INFRASTRUCTURE

ENERGY

South Africa attempted alternatives to oil long before the OPEC squeeze began. As early as 1950 it started with the manufacturing of oil from coal — utilising its abundant supply of low-grade coal to compensate for its total lack in oil resources.

Sasol

The South African Coal, Oil and Gas Corporation (SASOL) began commercial production of liquid fuels from coal in 1955 at SASOL I. Since then it has been supplying up to thirteen percent of South Africa's fuel needs in this manner. Once SASOL II and III, constructed at a combined cost of 7 billion dollars, are on stream, oil from coal will supply more than half of South Africa's fuel needs.

The apparent South African success in converting coal to oil has led to considerable interest in several developed countries with coal supplies of their own. Expectations are that some may acquire and incorporate the South African process to help meet the energy crunch. In the meantime South Africa runs the world's only commercial coal liquification and gasification plants. These plants, incidentally, spawned a large petro-chemical satellite industry. Also in operation in South Africa is the world's only modern coal-based methanol plant.

Other ways

Electricity in South Africa is also mostly dependent on coal burning. Nearly ninety percent of the electric power output is coal-based, while in recent years several major hydro-electric projects have been developed.

Having developed its own uranium enrichment process and a substantial producer of this mineral — mostly as a by-product of gold — South Africa started construction in 1978 on its first nuclear power station at

Koeberg, near Cape Town. It is expected to come into operation around 1983.

Electricity in South Africa is almost exclusively managed and controlled by the Electricity Supply Commission (ESCOM) — like SASOL a government controlled corporation.

Its large exports of both coal and uranium and the use of these alternative energy sources enable South Africa to earn more from these exports than it has to spend on oil imports.

Experimental
In the experimental stage is the use of sunflower oil as a substitute for diesel in agricultural machinery — some call it "flower power". Also, as elsewhere there is continued testing of methanol and ethanol (ethyl alcohol), obtained from fermentation and distillation of vegetable matter such as sugar cane, maize and even wood shavings.

Its sunny climate makes South Africa well suited to solar energy experimentation and more than thirty companies are already involved in manufacturing and maintaining solar water heaters.

In Natal, South Africa's major sugar growing area, motorists have been driving for more than fifty years on Union Spirit, manufactured from sugar cane.

Energy control
Energy in South Africa is the purview of the Department of Environmental Planning and Energy, Private Bag X213, Pretoria 0001. This country is attentive to any practical suggestions in this field, but chances are that overseas entrepreneurs will find more to buy than to sell. Ever since 1950 when it began to accept the fact that oil was one substance absent in its almost complete arsenal of minerals, South Africa had been devising new ways of generating energy.

Oil
The search for oil is still on under the direction of the Southern Oil Exploration Corporation (SOEKOR), a State-financed company. Participation from overseas is welcomed, but as yet no real meaningful strikes have occured apart from a large natural gas find forty miles off-shore. Still, several large overseas companies remain active in this search for oil.

WE FOUND COAL AND STRUCK OIL

You cannot separate "energy" and "crisis" – either in today's world or tomorrow's. While South Africa continues its search for oil, Sasol is expanding its highly successful oil-from-coal operations.

Starting from scratch in 1950, Sasol soon proved it could produce oil from coal economically by declaring a profit only five years after commissioning Sasol One. This profitability has been handsomely increased ever since.

Not only were formidable technological problems successfully overcome: economic viability was achieved within the strict discipline of a profit-orientated free market environment where cost efficiency and product quality are decisive.

Today, Sasol One is the only commercially proven oil-from-coal plant in the world. Sasol Two, costing more than $3 billion, commenced production early in 1980. Sasol

Three, announced in February 1979 and now under construction at an estimated cost of $4 billion, will complete the present expansion of Sasol's synfuel production capacity.

Together, these three plants will convert more than 32 million tons of low-grade coal per year into liquid fuels, pipeline gas and chemicals, bringing the goal of energy self-sufficiency significantly closer to reality.

These products will be produced at prices commercially competitive with those derived from crude oil – a unique achievement placing South Africa in the forefront of the urgent search for alternative energy sources.

Sasol – a proud pioneer in the successful application of tomorrow's technology to the energy needs of today.

Sasol

P.O. Box 1, Sasolburg, 9570, Republic of South Africa.

de Villiers and Company 72161

SASOL PROCESS

The SASOL fuels-from-coal process is a two-stage, indirect liquefaction technique. It can be tailored to a broad range of product slates, depending on the needs of the markets to be served. Among its advantages are its ability to use lower quality coals and a long history of successful operating experience.

The process works like this: Coal from the mine is crushed, sized, and separated. The finer coal, which would retard the efficiency of the Lurgi gasifiers, becomes fuel for the steam generating plant. The coarser coal, along with steam and oxygen from the air-separation plant, are channeled into a Lurgi gasifier. At a pressure of about 30 atmospheres, the coal reacts with the steam and oxygen.

In addition to raw synthesis gas, the reactors produce tar, oils and gas liquids. The tars and oils are refined into tar products. The gas liquids are treated in a Phenosolvan process to produce phenols and ammonia.

The raw gas is purified in a Rectisol unit, which separates out carbon dioxide and hydrogen sulfide, leaving a pure synthesis gas containing 85 percent hydrogen and carbon monoxide, 13 percent methane and 2 percent residual nitrogen and carbon dioxide.

In the second liquefaction stage, or "Synthol" stage, the synthesis gas is reacted with any of several iron-based catalysts in SASOL Fischer-Tropsch fluid-bed reactors.

In a subsequent product recovery stage, hydrogen and light hydrocarbons, including methane, are separated from the stream of Fischer-Tropsch products. Although methane can of course be sold as pipeline gas, SASOL uses a methane reforming stage in which oxygen and steam are added to the methane in a heated, pressurized reactor to form hydrogen and carbon monoxide. These products are then recycled into the synthesis-gas steam as feedstock to the synthol unit.

Downstream, a product refinery produces hydrocarbon products, which include LPG, gasoline, diesel fuel, fuel oil, jet fuel, and a variety of chemicals. The ratio between primary products such as gasoline and diesel fuel can be varied at will from 80-20 to 50-50 to suit local needs. This is done by varying the special-purpose catalysts in the Fischer-Tropsch reactors and with suitable adjustments to primary processing facilities.

SHIPPING

South Africa lives on main street as far as shipping is concerned. More than sixty percent of the Western world's oil traffic goes past its front doorstep. On an average some thirteen thousand vessels call at its ports every year.

Those who wish to engage in trade from or with South Africa, will find no problems in moving bulk. Harbour facilities are modern and complete, while dozens of shipping lines provide sailings to all four corners of the globe.

Harbour

With the exception of stevedoring at its major ports, all other services at South Africa's harbours such as pilotage, tugs, berthing, discharging and the like, are under government control. This ensures, for one, proper co-ordination with the railroads feeding these harbours with freight from inland areas as both are operated by the South African Railway and Harbour Administration.

Those interested in a comprehensive check list of costs involved in wharfage, shipping, sorting, weighing and measuring, storage, and marking of freight, need only consult the *SAR and H Official Harbour Tariff Book of Dues and Charges* — unless they prefer the easier way of leaving it to the professionals. There are an adequate number of shipping agents handling this side of affairs at all major centres in South Africa — and everyone, of course, maintains corresponding overseas offices.

Major ports

These are the six major ports:

★ **Durban:** It is not only the largest harbour in South Africa itself, but in Africa, handling close to forty million tons of freight per year. It is fully equipped to handle deep sea containers and general cargo and has grain elevators and pre-cooling facilities for fruit and other exports. Three oil pipe lines feed crude and refined oil inland from Durban.

★ **Cape Town:** Often referred to as Table Bay, this port is fully equipped with deep-sea container and pre-cooling facilities as well as grain elevators.

★ **Port Elizabeth:** As in the case of Cape Town and Durban fully equipped with pre-cooling, container and grain facilities. Mostly used for mineral and wool exports.

★ **Richards Bay:** This harbour, two hundred kilometers north of Durban, was developed recently to handle mostly bulk mineral exports such as coal, but it is also capable of handling general cargo.

★ **Saldanha Bay:** A recently developed harbour one hundred kilometres north of Cape Town, mainly for bulk mineral exports such as iron ore.

★ **East London:** River port with pre-cooling facilities and grain elevators.

Apart from its own ports, South Africa still has continued use of Maputo (formerly Lourenco Marques) in Mocambique. This harbour, which serves to handle excess freight from South Africa, is naturally under control of the Mocambique authorities and those who wish to use this alternative route should determine space availability, dues and charges separately beforehand.

Shipping Lines

South Africa has two major shipping lines of its own — Safmarine and Unicorn — providing extensive services around its three thousand kilometre coastline and to overseas ports. Safmarine has a fleet of some forty vessels, including newly built fully cellular container ships, refrigeration vessels, oil tankers and ore carriers. It provides sailings to the Americas, the Caribbean, Europe, Australia and the Far East. In the United States alone Safmarine calls at twelve ports — among others New York, Philadelphia, Baltimore, Charleston, Savannah, Jacksonville, Houston and New Orleans.

Regular world-wide services are also provided by many other shipping lines, including Moore-McCormack Lines, Hellenic Lines, Deutsche Ost-Afrika Linien, Lloyd Triestino, K Line, Gold Star Line, Nippon Yusen Kaisha, Mitsui OSK Lines and Union Castle Line.

AIR TRANSPORT

Frequent freight and passenger air services operate between South Africa and major centres abroad. There are daily flights from fourteen points in Europe, five direct flights each week from the United States, five services weekly from South America and two from Australia, as well as four a week from the Far East.

International services

Sixteen airlines operate between South Africa and destinations overseas: South African Airways, Aerolineas Argentinas, Alitalia Airlines, British Airways, El Al Israel Airlines, the Royal Dutch Airlines (KLM), Iberia International Airlines, Lufthansa German Airlines, Luxavia Airlines, Olympic Airways, Sabena Belgian World Airlines, Scandinavian Airlines System (SAS), Swissair, Transportes Aereos Porugueses (TAP), Union des Transport Aeriens (UTA French Airlines) and Varig Brazilian Airlines.

Together these airlines provide on an average well over fourteen thousand seats per week on some seventy flights from thirty-three points abroad to South Africa.

Neighbouring States

There are also regular services between South Africa and its neighbours such as Botswana, Swaziland and Zimbabwe. These routes are handled by Air Botswana, DETA (Mocambique Airlines), Air Malawi, Air Mauritius, Air Zimbabwe, Swazi Air, Transkei Airways and Suidwes Lugdiens (SWA/Namibia).

Domestic Services

South African Airways, the national carrier, also happens to be the sole authorised scheduled operator between eleven major airports within the country. Despite this monopoly, SAA insists on maintaining the same high standards that have become its hallmark internationally where competition is stiff.

Wide-bodied aircraft are increasingly used, supplemented with Boeing 727's and 737's as well as 707's. Flights are frequent enough to allow businessmen pressed for time, a tight itinerary between major points in South Africa. Each week, for example, there are 61 round trips between Johannesburg and Cape Town.

Charter Services

Those whose business or pleasure requires swift travel to remote points in South Africa, have a choice of charter services. There are some 150 pilots licensed to provide non-scheduled or charter services from eighty airfields throughout the country. They use a wide variety of craft ranging from small single-engined two-seaters to all-weather executive jets.

The Golden Link to the Land of Gold.

Gold bullion, Golden Sunshine, Golden beaches, Golden-hearted people . . . that's South Africa. And South African Airways is the Golden Airline which flies you there from five continents.

Fast DIRECT services from London and Europe – the highest frequency of any airline – with many flights NON-STOP.

Fast DIRECT services from New York – 5 times a week.

Fast DIRECT services from Sydney and Perth.

Fast DIRECT services from South America, Taiwan and Hong Kong.

In extra-spacious Boeing 747's – with luxurious STRATOSLEEPER seats in First Class.

And whatever the price of gold, our service will never, ever go off the Gold Standard.

SAA
South African Airways
Where no-one's a stranger

SAA5438 LS-FCE

Entry

Point of entry to South Africa by air is usually Jan Smuts Airport, near Johannesburg. Two other major airports handling traffic from abroad are D.F. Malan Airport near Cape Town, and Louis Botha Airport near Durban. (All the major airports except East London's are named after former South African Prime Ministers).

Also equipped to take care of customs formalities are smaller airports such as Rand Airport, Komatipoort, Messina, Wonderboom and Lanseria, where charter and private aircraft often first arrive from points abroad.

ROAD TRANSPORT

Apart from rail transport, the South African Railways also provides road transport services for both freight and passengers. Private trucking companies are, however, responsible for much of the road freight hauling between major centres in South Africa.

The entrepreneur has a wide choice of companies when it comes to assigning freight, unless regulations require that SAR be the carrier. There are a few instances where such rules apply in order to make it feasible for SAR to maintain uneconomic but necessary services in areas shunned by private enterprise.

Johannesburg Stock Exchange

THE PROFITABLE TRADE LINK

Ranked 155 in Fortune's list of the 500 largest companies outside the U.S., Barlow Rand Limited is South Africa's largest industrial corporation in terms of sales, total assets, net income and market capitalisation – and has a long record of consistently outstanding performance.

Through our 250 trading companies, the group is widely diversified with a broad manufacturing base, having strong interests in earthmoving and mechanical handling equipment; ferro-alloy and stainless steel production, electrical and general engineering; building materials and steel distribution; electronics; household appliances; sugar; textiles; packaging and paper; automobile distribution; paint; cement and lime; property – and has enjoyed long standing ties with 8 of Fortune's top 100 U.S. companies, plus many other well-known international corporations.

In addition, with our extensive mining interests, Barlow Rand is a major South African exporter of coal, chrome, asbestos, fluorspar and other important base minerals – plus gold and uranium.

Employing over 193 000 people, Barlow Rand's policy is one of equal benefits and opportunities for all and a firm commitment to improve their quality of life both at work and at home.

If you feel there could be profit opportunities for your company in Southern Africa and would like to know more about us, write for further information to: Group Public Relations Co-ordinator, Barlow Rand Limited, P.O. Box 4862, Johannesburg 2000 – South Africa.

Could be we're the profitable link you're looking for.

Barlow Rand Limited

5490 LS-FCB

RAIL TRANSPORT

As in other parts of the new world, railway tracks in South Africa follow-ed in the footsteps of the pioneers as they pushed inland. Today this rail network touches every corner of the country and carries bulk shipments of coal, ore, grain, timber, and fruit for export to the major ports. Container trains run regularly between a depot at City Deep, near Johannesburg, and Durban.

State control

South African Railways is under state control. This helps it to operate at reasonable rates with subsidies as private systems elsewhere in the world are coming to a grinding halt under severe economic pressures.

Modernization

While other railroads across the world went out of business, the South African Railways actually expanded and modernized to meet the new demands of a rapidly increasing flow of export minerals and materials from the interior to its ports. The only alteration that it did not make in recent years was to change the gauge of its tracks — at 1 065mm quite narrow by normal standards.

Steam

South Africa used to be a mecca for steam engine buffs from all over the world. An abundant supply of cheap coal made steam-driven locomotives still feasible long after they were phased out elsewhere in the industrialised world.

Eventually the high operating cost of these romantic puffing dragons, also caught up with South Africa. A switch to electricity and diesel-electric traction is now almost complete and steam engines are mostly seen in shunting yards — some still barely used for shunting while others stand silently, rusting away.

Blue Train

Still attracting visitors from abroad in large numbers is South Africa's luxurious Blue Train service between Cape Town and Johannesburg. Rated among the very top few by world experts, this train provides a very special diversion for businessmen who wish to mix pleasure with work — and had the good sense to make reservations months ahead. It is near impossible to get on in under three months prior notice, unless there are cancellations or very special circumstances.

The Blue Train operates twice weekly in summer and once a week in winter, both directions, between Pretoria and Cape Town. It is an overnight journey of 1 608km. During the special holiday season — beginning December until mid-January — this service extends to three trips in each direction every week.

Those who are determined to get a feel of South Africa's first-rate rail passenger services and did not manage to get accommodations on the Blue Train, have other somewhat less opulent but still exotic options: The Drakensberg runs twice weekly between Johannesburg and Durban (785km) and once a week between Durban and Cape Town (2 091km); the Trans-Natal, an overnight express between Johannesburg and Durban, which runs daily in each direction; the Trans-Karoo, which operates five times a week in each direction between Cape Town and Johannesburg (1 553km); and the Orange Express, twice a week in each direction between Cape Town and Durban.

We're NO.1 & NO.2

Wang is the largest in sales of screen-based Word Processing Systems, and the second largest in sales of small business computers in South Africa and the world. When in South Africa, do as the South Africans do. Speak to General Business Systems.

Largest Wang representative worldwide

HEAD OFFICE: BOX 41268 · CRAIGHALL 2024 · TELEX 424847 · TEL: 789-1912 · BRANCHES THROUGHOUT SOUTH AFRICA

COMMUNICATIONS

The South African Post Office handles all that country's communications, internal as well as overseas. Postal services, telecommunications as well as data transmission facilities are all provided under one roof.

Especially since 1968 when the Post Office switched to business practices instead of functioning purely as a government department, efficiency in all areas of communication has increased considerably. South Africa prides itself in having one of the very best in overseas telephone links — a claim usually endorsed by seasoned travellers.

Postal Services

At more than two thousand post offices customers can count on a total range of letter and parcel services, ranging from registered to certified mail, cash on delivery (COD), insured and express delivery to priority mail service. As in all developed countries there is a business reply service available for companies wishing to mass mail prepaid reply cards to potential customers.

Urgent overseas mail

Urgent overseas airmail can be handed in at the post office at Jan Smuts Airport, near Johannesburg, until two hours before departure of the flight for which they are scheduled. The postal authorities will assure that they make this flight at a small extra fee.

This service is, however, limited to ordinary letters and does not provide for parcels, express and registered articles. There are private agencies in Johannesburg which undertake urgent door-to-door delivery of such items destined for overseas points. A speedy and reliable priority mail service is available from the eight largest post offices to Great Britain, Hong Kong and Taiwan.

Philatelic Services

Stamp collectors will find South Africa in the major league as far as frequency and quality of special stamp issues are concerned. A special philatelic service is provided by the Post Office which, apart from over the counter sales, operates an extensive mail order service to more than twenty-six thousand collectors world-wide.

This service also includes stamps issued by South-West Africa/Namibia and black states such as Venda, Bophuthatswana and Transkei.

Collectors who wish to be placed on the mailing list or to establish a deposit account with this agency, need to write to: The Director, Philatelic Services, Private Bag X505, Pretoria 0001, South Africa.

Telex services

Some nineteen thousand telex subscribers in South Africa are linked through eight automatic exchanges with subscribers in ninety-seven other countries, while another ninety-three countries can be reached by way of a manual international telex exchange in Johannesburg.

Data transmission

Data transmission was first introduced in South Africa in the mid-sixties and updated regularly since. Today the businessman in South Africa can count on local and overseas transmissions systems comparable to that available anywhere else in the world.

Telephone services

Dialling to many overseas countries from South Africa is direct and swift thanks to elaborate cable and satellite links. Direct dialling also exists between all South Africa's major centres and some of its smaller towns and hamlets.

Chapter 4

FINANCE

BANKING

South Africa's banking system originated in Britain and was at first dominated by British banks. Today there are several homegrown giants dominating much of the banking scene in South Africa — rated as one of the most sophisticated in the world.

Reserve Bank

At the centre of South Africa's banking and financing is the *Reserve Bank* with its head office in Pretoria and branches in all the country's major cities.

The South African Reserve Bank is both locally and internationally an agent and advisor for its government. As keeper of the country's gold and foreign reserves it is the sole issuer of banknotes; provides clearing facilities for the private banking sector; sets the official bank rate; regulates together with the South African Treasury the purchase and sale of government stock and bills; sets liquid assets and reserve requirements for private banks; and regulates exchange control.

Gold bullion

As the only authorised buyer of gold bullion in South Africa, the Reserve Bank also acts as sales agent for that country's gold mining industry abroad. At the International Monetary Fund in Washington in the past, the South African delegation has always argued strongly in favour of an international monetary system based on gold and there is no reason to expect any change in this approach as long as their country remains the world's major producer of this precious metal. Chances are that South Africa will remain number one in this area until at least the end of this century.

South Africa is a founder member of the IMF, as well as the World Bank, the International Finance Corporation, and the International Development Association (IDA). Of late its membership in all these organisations has been tenuous as a result of political agitation by nations opposed to its so-called apartheid policy.

63

Private banking

The private banking sector provides the foreign entrepreneur with a comprehensive, sophisticated and properly regulated service. The number of banking institutions in South Africa is strictly regulated to prevent overbanking. Applicants who wish to establish new banking institutions are required by the Registrar of Banks to prove public need before such applications are considered.

Overseas businessmen will most likely deal indirectly through their own banks, and once they are familiar with South Africa, directly, with several types of South African banking institutions: commercial banks, merchant banks, acceptance and discount houses. Other financial institutions such as general banks, building societies, hire purchase and savings banks are more specifically geared to the domestic market.

Commercial banks

There are nine commercial banks in South Africa offering through a network of more than 7000 branches a complete range of financial and related services in South Africa, South West Africa/Namibia and — in some cases — other territories in the Rand Monetary Area. Most South African banks have links with foreign banks.

Although commercial banks are mostly associated with short-term financing and checking facilities, some have in recent years ventured into medium-term credit for commerce and industry. These banks, incidentally, obtain most of their funds (more than 60%) through savings and time deposits.

Merchant banks

Modelled on their British counterparts, South African merchant banks and acceptance houses deal with a small number of large depositors and apart from a few regional offices have no branch system.

In merchant banks, instead of pure banking operations, the emphasis is on full capital market services. Serving as financial intermediaries, these merchant banks assist companies and individuals with equity and loan participation plans, medium term loans and bridging finance. They provide experts services in banking, the local money market, foreign exchange, import and export financing and lending.

These institutions are also as corporate financial advisors fully conversant with stock exchange procedures and rules, company law, tax law, accounting practices in South Africa, funding sources, the techniques of merging and acquisitions, new issues, and the like.

Discount houses

There are only three such institutions registered. Working on an understanding with the Reserve Bank, these discount houses specialise in mobilising call money, which in turn is converted into short-term official and non-official paper.

Credit

Although a wide range of financing and credit is available in South Africa, the foreign entrepreneur needs to be cautioned. Local borrowing facilities are not freely available to companies with a foreign ownership of twenty-five percent or more. The permissable level of borrowing is actually directly related to the proportion of local ownership. However, exceptional sympathetic treatment is generally accorded specifically approved projects. (See also LOCAL BORROWING).

There is one golden rule in dealing with South Africa: Always remember that this country welcomes the foreign entrepreneur for two reasons: money and know-how. If he brings both he will find himself feted and favoured.

EXCHANGE CONTROL

Any foreigner doing business with South Africa should keep in mind that exchange control regulations affect all transactions with the Rand Monetary Area. This area, which uses the Rand as its legal currency, comprises South Africa, South West Africa/Namibia, Lesotho, Swaziland, Transkei, Bophuthatswana, and Venda.

While the twenty-two Exchange Control Regulations in effect between the Rand Monetary Area and the outside world are closely monitored for contraventions, Exchange Control is designed to encourage investment from abroad and can actually serve to favour foreigners doing business with the Rand Monetary Area.

The Rand Monetary Area makes a clear distinction between two types of Rand: Commercial Rand and Financial Rand. There are not two sets of banknotes. The terms simply refer to two different rates in purchasing Rand with foreign currency.

Commercial Rand

Foreign funds transferred to the Rand Monetary Area through normal banking channels at the current Commercial Rand rate, can be invested at any local bank on call or in a fixed deposit account, without any restrictions. The Rand Monetary Area bank concerned will classify these as Non-Resident Accounts and as long as these funds remain in the banking sector, they are freely transferable anywhere in the world. Also the interest on these bank deposits is freely transferable, subject only to a 10% non-resident tax.

As soon as the Non-Resident Account holder, however, invests funds in the Rand Monetary Area outside the banking sector, such funds are eligible to be converted into Financial Rands — giving the foreigner a more favourable conversion rate than the Commercial Rand rate.

Financial Rand

In certain cases foreign investors are entitled to the Financial Rand rate in the Rand Monetary Area instead of having to rely on the Commercial Rand rate, gaining a decided advantage as the Financial Rand is usually sold at a rate substantially lower than that of the Commercial Rand. Also holders of Non-Resident Accounts with their foreign currency already converted into Commercial Rand are entitled to convert again to Financial Rand for certain investments outside the banking sector.

The difference between the exchange rate of the Commercial and Financial Rand fluctuates considerably. It is, however, evident that the Financial Rand will remain for the forseeable future cheaper to the foreign investor than the Commercial Rand.

At the beginning of 1979, for example, the price of the Financial Rand stood at US $0.64 per Rand, representing a discount of approximately 44% on the current commercial exchange rate of 1 Rand = US $1.15. A year later the Commercial Rand rate was US $1.2390 in comparison with a Financial Rand rate of US $0.92 — amounting to a 25% difference.

Foreign investments

Foreign entrepreneurs who wish to take advantage of the Financial Rand rate in establishing themselves in the Rand Monetary Area are required to obtain prior approval from the South African Reserve Bank. Such applications have to be channeled to this central bank through the entrepreneur's own bank. Every application is treated on its own merit, but the Reserve Bank has indicated that it will give preferential treatment to Financial Rand investments in commercial and industrial enterprises which will benefit the Rand Monetary Area one of the following ways:

(a) Expand manufacturing capacity;
(b) promote exports;
(c) provide labour in manpower surplus areas;
(d) develop strategic industries;
(e) introduce fresh foreign know-how;
(f) are labour intensive;
(g) and serve to replace imports.

Transfer of earnings on such Financial Rand capital investments and dividends on shares bought with Financial Rand are allowed at normal Commercial Rand rates, subject of course to prevailing taxes. Should a non-resident, however, wish to repatriate his capital investment, he is obliged to do so in terms of Financial Rand.

Foreign shares

Financial Rand is especially useful to foreign buyers of shares quoted on the Johannesburg Stock Exchange. Renowned brokerage houses abroad deal in several of these, mostly gold and mining shares, while transfers for purchases of JSE shares not listed abroad, can be handled through commercial banks.

More recently the South African Reserve Bank has also allowed Financial Rand transactions to foreigners buying shares in South African companies not quoted on the Johannesburg Stock Exchange — as well as in the purchasing of property. In such cases, however, specific prior approval has to be obtained from the Reserve Bank.

In all share transactions involving Financial Rands foreign investors stand to gain — or lose — depending on the going rate of the Financial Rand itself. It is therefore advisable to consider in such transactions not only the current value and expected rise of the share involved, but also the ruling rate of exchange for Financial Rand. A decline or increase in the FR rate can often mean more in profits — or losses — to the foreign investor than the fluctuation in the value of the share itself.

Exchange control in South Africa can be a pitfall or a windfall to the foreign businessman, depending on his approach. His first step should be to acquaint himself with existing rules and rates. The best way to do so is through a reputable bank with a well-structured international division — preferably one that has regular contact with a South African banking institution or its own branches or subsidiaries in that country.

LOCAL BORROWING

South Africa is interested in foreign enterprises with capital and know-how and goes a long way in attracting them with tax concessions and other incentives. It is less enthusiastic about those who come with empty hands and wish to borrow locally for new business ventures.

Still, foreign-owned companies operating in South Africa are not precluded from borrowing once they have obtained the necessary approval from the Reserve Bank. Incidentally, all companies in South Africa with a foreign ownership of 25% or more have to obtain such prior permission from the central bank.

If a company in South Africa is 100% foreign owned, its borrowing will be restricted to 25% of its effective capital. Under *effective capital* items such as paid-up share capital, reserves built up from profits, and approved loans from parent companies are included.

The size of the South African participation in such foreign held local companies directly influences their borrowing powers. The formula used for determining a partly South African held foreign-owned company is as follows:

$$25\% \; + \; \frac{\text{Percentage of South African interest}}{\text{Percentage of foreign interest}} \; \times \; 25$$

If, for example, 40% of the interest in a particular company is held by South Africans and 60% by foreigners, the firm will be able to borrow locally:

$$25\% \; + \; \frac{40}{60} \times 25 \; = \; 25 \; + \; 16.66 \; = \; 41.66\%$$

Under certain special circumstances foreign entrepreneurs may find the South African authorities more amenable to local borrowing and quite willing to relax normal restrictions. Foreign-held companies which operate, for example, in one of the decentralised or economic development areas, will find the authorities anxious to facilitate additional borrowing for expansion. (See DECENTRALISATION INCENTIVES).

TAXES

The foreign investor will find taxes in South Africa neither exhorbitant nor unusually low. The basic rate for companies happens to be quite normal at 40% plus a surcharge of 5%, adding up to 42% of all taxable income.

As elsewhere in the world, however, the true measure of taxes in South Africa lies not in the basic rate, but the scope of the deductions and concessions offered by the authorities. In this respect the foreigner will find South Africa an attractive proposition.

South Africa has a long-standing policy of encouraging foreign investment at considerable initial cost to itself in the form of special incentives. It has evidently paid off considering the steady growth in foreign investment despite severe political pressures in recent years. (See DISINVESTMENT PRESSURES and FOREIGN INVESTMENT).

Apart from the basic rate, foreign companies and individuals are subject to the following taxes:

Undistributed Profits Tax

Normally foreign companies doing business in South Africa pay an undistributed profits tax of 33⅓% on distributable income not paid out in dividends. There are, however, exemptions such as companies where the majority of the shares are held by foreign individuals or in certain cases where such profits are ploughed back into operations.

Non-Resident Shareholders' Tax

Dividends paid to non-residents are exempt from normal tax but subject to a so-called Non-Resident Shareholders' Tax of 15%. This is applicable to both individuals and foreign companies.

Non-Resident Tax on Interest

Non-residents — both individuals and companies — earning interest through loans to persons or companies in South Africa are liable to a 10% tax. The lenders have little choice in the matter as the debtor is required to withhold the tax. If, however, the debtor can convince the authorities *beforehand* that such a loan is to be used for long-term industrial or mining development in South Africa, the foreign lender may be exempted from this 10% tax. Also in cases where a lender is liable to pay taxes in his own country without receiving credit for the 10% already remitted, exemptions are granted.

Double taxation is in any event something that should not concern everybody in dealing with South Africa — only some. The following countries have *comprehensive agreements* with South Africa to prevent double taxation: The United States, United Kingdom, Germany, Canada, Switzerland, The Netherlands and Sweden.

71

In the case of countries such as Belgium, Brazil, Denmark, France, Israel, Italy, Ireland, Norway, Spain and Greece more *limited agreements* are in effect, restricted to the avoidance of double taxation on profits derived from shipping and air transport.

Royalties Tax

Non-resident individuals and foreign companies are liable to pay a tax of 42% on 30% of the gross amount derived from royalties in South Africa.* Once again such individuals and companies are allowed a rebate on taxes paid in the same respect in their own countries.

Employee's Tax

Non-residents receiving "remuneration" from South African sources are subject to a withholding tax. The authorities define *remuneration* in broad terms to include among other items salary, leave pay, allowances, overtime pay, bonuses, gratuities, commissions, fees, pensions, annuities, allowances and the like.

Directors' fees paid by a public company to any person who is not resident in South Africa are also subject to employee's tax, while non-resident directors receiving fees from private companies are not obliged to pay such taxes.

These are some of the more important taxes concerning the foreign investor in South Africa. As already indicated, however, tax rates in themselves hardly tell the full story in most countries, including South Africa. Equally important are the *deductions* and *concessions* allowed by the authorities.

In this respect the prospective foreign investor will find South Africa remarkably generous in its pursuit of overseas capital and know-how.

Tax Allowances

Apart from a special exporters allowance to industries selling goods manufactured in South Africa overseas, a wide range of other tax deductions and concessions apply to manufacturing plants.

The South African authorities actually distinguish between new industries in existing industrial complexes and new plants in the so-called *economic development areas.* These are areas bordering the traditional tribal or black homelands where an abundance of labour exists coupled with a dire need for industrialisation — as opposed to industrialised areas such as the so-called Pretoria/Witwatersrand/Vereeniging triangle around Johannesburg.

While the tax concessions granted to new industries in the existing industrial areas of South Africa are impressive by any standards, the

* Amounting in effect to 12.6% of the total amount.

allowances made to those who venture into the economic development areas, in and around the black national states, are unusual.

Manufacturers in industrialised areas, apart from the general deduction allowed to all businesses for expenditures and losses incurred in the production of income, are entitled to special deductions for:

★ Wear and tear.
★ Initial investment in plant and machinery.
★ Buildings and improvements.
★ Training of employees.
★ Housing of employees.
★ Lease premiums.

Those who establish themselves in the economic development areas can expect a whole range of extra tax and other incentives. This is discussed separately under ESTABLISHING A FACTORY and DECENTRALISATION INCENTIVES.

Changes

According to the pundits, there is nothing quite as certain as death and taxes. They forgot to make one important distinction:

Whereas death is bound to remain the same, taxes do change from one year to another. Although this general outline on taxes in South Africa may remain valid, actual rates and percentages will not. Prospective foreign investors will presumably obtain the latest and more detailed information before they make up their minds on whether to expand to South Africa.

Incidentally, there is no capital gains tax in South Africa.

Those who wish to contact the Receiver of Revenue directly for further information should address their letters to any of its offices in major cities such as Pretoria, Johannesburg, Cape Town or Bloemfontein. No box number or street address is needed. And if the letter is sent from any point within South Africa, no postage either.

Chapter 5

INVESTMENT

FOREIGN INVESTMENT

For at least fifteen years until 1975 South Africa's gross domestic product grew at an average annual rate of 6 percent. Foreign capital, it is estimated, generated about 2 percent or one-third of that growth.

Despite occasional politically inspired pronouncements by responsible men that South Africa does not really need foreign capital, the opposite remains true. Notwithstanding the large increase in the price of gold and the billions that it brought, South Africa continues to make it as attractive as possible for investors — a sure sign that it not only needs but actively solicits foreign capital and direct investment.

Foreigners are enticed by the following:

Assured repatriation of dividends and current earnings on ventures, numerous concessions to companies interested in establishing operations in government-designated growth areas (including low-interest loans), preferential transportation rates, and cash rebates and tax concessions. Profits are usually much higher than elsewhere in the developed world and in itself serve to encourage investment. (See also ESTABLISHING A FACTORY, DECENTRALISATION INCENTIVES, TAXES, and PROFITS).

Foreign holdings

European and American investors dominate the South African foreign-business community scene. British assets in South Africa are estimated at $12 billion of which $6.8 billion are in direct assets and $5.1 billion in shares. The British holding is about half of all foreign investment in South Africa. The United States accounts for $1.8 billion in direct investment and some $2 billion in shares — mostly mining. This gives the United States approximately 17 percent of the foreign investment total in South Africa. The remaining third comes almost entirely from the European Economic Community or sterling block countries. Japan, an extensive trader with South Africa, does most of its business by way of licensing agreements instead of investment.

There are more than 2 000 overseas companies with direct investment and operations in South Africa. Britain leads the way with 1 200, followed by the United States and West Germany with 350 each. Other notable investing countries are France and Italy.

European and American banks have also supplied most of South Africa's overseas loans in recent years. Its demand for such facilities from abroad dramatically decreased with the sharp upturn in the price of gold at the beginning of the eighties, but loans are still sought from time to time.

Foreign investment in the past centred mostly on the following sectors: Mining, petroleum, coal, chemical, metals, automotive, textile, computer, electronics, and paper and pulp.

PROFITS

South Africans in their pitch for overseas investment never fail to mention profitability and stability as plus points. (See RISK FACTOR). Barring a short but severe recession in 1975, South Africa managed throughout the seventies to give investors among the highest returns on investment world-wide.

In 1969 the official *Statistical Abstract of the United States* calculated returns on American capital invested in the South African manufacturing industry at 9.5 percent — as against 5.7 percent in Western Europe, 5.1 percent in South America and 4.9 for all countries.

In the two years before 1975 some overseas companies averaged as high as 16 percent and more in returns. The U.S. Department of Commerce estimated returns on U.S. investment in South Africa at 18.6 percent in 1973 and 17.9 percent in 1974. (The 1974 rate of return on manufacturing operations worldwide was 13 percent in developing countries and in developed countries 12.4 percent).

After a slump due to the recession of 1975 (returns on all U.S. investment actually fell to 9 percent in South Africa as compared to 13 percent worldwide) recovery began in 1976. During that year returns went up again to 14 percent and remained steady until the end of 1978 when South Africa began to experience a remarkable upswing. Several computer and electronics manufacturers experienced expansion at a rate of 30 to 60 percent per year.

At the close of the seventies it was not only the gold price (both in bullion and shares) and Krugerrand sales that skyrocketed. Also other industrial activity and the South African economy in general reflected a boom, while most of the rest of the world suffered. The Johannesburg Stock Exchange in 1979 out-performed every other market in the world. (See JOHANNESBURG STOCK EXCHANGE).

REPATRIATION OF PROFITS

There is no restriction of transfer of profits, dividends or royalties to overseas principals, after tax. On the liquidation of a foreign owned local undertaking, however, fixed capital amounts are subject to Exchange control and repatriation is likely to be in terms of Financial Rand. (See EXCHANGE CONTROL and TAXES).

Companies or concerns with a foreign shareholding of 25% or more which have availed themselves of local borrowing facilities must also obtain Exchange Control approval prior to repatriation of profits and dividends. Normal trade credit, nonrecourse factoring and hire purchase facilities on non-productive items are not regarded as Local Borrowing. (See also LOCAL BORROWING).

Fees

Payment by South African companies to foreign associates or principals of fees for technical and managerial services is subject to Exchange Control. The authorities will need to be satisfied that the services incurred are necessary and not obtainable with equal facility in South Africa. Especially service fee payment by wholly-owned subsidiaries to their foreign parents comes under close scrutiny as the Reserve Bank prefers to see foreign investors withdrawing their profits from South Africa in the form of dividends instead.

Licence

Licencing and royalties, as in the case of fees paid overseas, need to be cleared with Exchange Control at the S.A. Reserve Bank after such agreements have been submitted to and approved by the Department of Industries. Once an agreement is approved by both parties, payments can be made through normal commercial banking channels in routine fashion.

In considering licencing and royalty agreements, the Department of Industries has no fixed formula. Every application is considered on its own merits. Applicants should, however, bear in mind that the following factors count:

★ Licence agreements in the consumer-good field are considered as meriting a lesser royalty than those in the capital goods field.
★ Licence agreements allowing the licensee to export to foreign countries with a large potential market justify a higher royalty rate.
★ Licence for new industries which will provide employment for large numbers of black workers in decentralised industrial areas justify higher royalty rates (See DECENTRALISATION INCENTIVES).
★ Lump-sum royalties and down payments are not encouraged.
★ If the agreement licences a package of rights — patents and trade marks and know-how — a single, total royalty figure is preferred (See PATENTS, TRADEMARKS and COPYRIGHT).

RISK FACTOR

Return on investment is hardly the only consideration when investing abroad. (See PROFITS).

Although risk pertains to more than the political, foreign investors usually seem to have this factor foremost in their minds when approaching South Africa. This is understandable. Apart from having on its borders several neighbours in uneasy stages of transition — some with Marxist regimes — South Africa contains the seeds of racial dissent and disorder within itself.

Racial pressures

For the past thirty years there were some in South Africa and abroad who insisted that it was only a matter of time before this country crumbled under racial pressures. These doom prophets at first gave South Africa a lease of life amounting to five years, then ten and today twenty and more.

At the same time there were those in and outside the country who displayed an unqualified belief in its capacity to withstand shocks from within and outside.

Between these two poles of pessimism and optimism there has always been a segment who maintained that nothing is gained anywhere without an element of risk. They were the ones who bought at bargain basement prices when racial clashes occurred in Sharpeville (1961) and SOWETO (1976) and others panicked and sold.

The debate over South Africa's future political stability is bound to continue — unless the apocalypse predicted by some, does occur. Chances are that South Africa will continue to experience sporadic unrest due not only to its own internal racial complexity but to influences from outside.

Evaluations

The foreign investor will obviously seek updated and comprehensive evaluations of political and economic risk factors in South Africa before he proceeds with any venture. In doing so he has a choice between several reputable independent firms overseas.

Naturally his choice will depend on the reliability of the sources on which these evaluating firms draw. Preferably their reports should include expert independent viewpoints in South Africa itself, backed up with real figures and solid facts, instead of simply summarising overseas opinions and gut feelings — often based on nothing more than prejudice and press reports.

Quantifying risk

One American firm attempted to quantify risk in forty-five countries — including South Africa. Considering factors such as political stability, nationalisation, inflation, balance of payments, economic growth, labour and productivity, transportation, credit, and bureaucratic delays, Business Environment Risk Index (BERI) rates these countries on a scale of 0 to 100.

Subdividing these countries into Low Risk (85-70), Moderate Risk (69-55), High Risk (54-40) and Excessive Risk (below 40), BERI's most recent assessment of South Africa was a 62.2. This placed it in the company of countries such as Norway, Australia, Sweden, Venezuela and Denmark, in the Moderate Risk range. (Although the scale ranges from 100 down to 0, figures in practice run from the 80's down to the 20's).

Creditworthiness

To establish regional risk ratings the Institutional Investor approached more than a hundred banks world-wide. These banks were asked to rate on a scale of ten the creditworthiness of countries and were specifically precluded from judging their own.

This is how South Africa performed in comparison with the rest of the African Continent, and globally, during 1979 and 1980.

Africa: Country Risk Rating*

Regional Rank 1980	1979	Country	Global Rank	Institutional Investor Credit Rating	Change
1	1	South Africa	32	62.5	+0.5
2	2	Libya	42	58.2	-1.8
3	3	Algeria	46	56.3	-2.3
4	4	Nigeria	49	54.3	+0.2
5	5	Tunisia	56	49.2	-0.8
6	6	Ivory Coast	58	47.7	-0.5
7	7	Kenya	62	45.0	-0.6
8	8	Morocco	64	43.5	-2.0
9	9	Liberia	69	39.6	-1.1
10	10	Republic of Gabon	73	34.4	+1.1
11	11	Senegal	77	28.9	+0.4
12	14	Zimbabwe-Rhodesia	80	23.5	-0.3
13	12	Seychelles	81	21.8	-3.4
14	13	Tanzania	81	21.8	-3.2
15	16	Angola	85	19.0	-2.6
16	15	Sierra Leone	86	18.9	-3.7
17	17	Zambia	87	18.4	-2.3
18	19	Sudan	89	14.2	-4.3
19	18	Congo	90	14.0	-5.5
20	20	Ethiopia	91	12.1	-1.7
21	22	Uganda	95	8.3	-0.4
22	21	Zaire	96	7.5	-2.3
		Regional average rating		31.8	-1.6

* The higher the rank, the better the investment potential.

Source: Institutional Investor March, 1980.

79

Economic prospects

As the eighties arrived, South Africa experienced some political unrest coupled with promising economic prospects. Largely as a result of a dramatic rise in the price of gold, South Africa's economy showed an upturn while the world suffered.

The British National Institute of Economic and Social Research, for example, envisaged a real growth rate for South Africa of between 4 and 5.5 percent — the highest for any developed country except Japan. The International Monetary Fund, describing the world economic picture as "rather grim", anticipated a real output growth of 5 percent in South Africa.

Official claims

These assessments fell even slightly short of South Africa's official expectations of a growth rate of 7 percent in real gross domestic product. Traditionally the South African authorities tend to be conservative in their estimates — available from either the South African Reserve Bank, P.O. Box 427, Pretoria 0001 (Tel: 41 3011) or one of the following sources:

Office of the Economic Advisor
to the Prime Minister
Steyn's Building
270 Schoeman Street
Private Bag X455
Pretoria 0001

Department of Finance
Union Buildings
Private Bag X115
Pretoria 0001
Telegraphic: FINDEP

Government literature rarely fails to point out that there has never been nationalisation of private operations — local or foreign — in South Africa. Indeed, in enticing foreign business to establish operations in one of its own traditional black states, South Africa guarantees such firms against any takeover by these emerging states. (DECENTRALISATION INCENTIVES)

ESTABLISHING A COMPANY

What is in a name? Quite a lot when it comes to company names in South Africa. If a firm's name contains only the word *Limited* or *Ltd* it indicates that it is a *public company.* If on the other hand it is denoted as *Proprietary Limited* or *(Pty) Ltd,* it means that it is a private company. And, finally, if it contains the description *South Africa* or *SA,* it often indicates that this company is a subsidiary or an affiliate of an overseas corporation or parent company with the same name.

Registrar of Companies

Company names have to be approved by the Registrar of Companies, which has drawn up for the convenience of prospective applicants a special directive. This directive contains a detailed list of names that are considered to be misleading and undesirable. Still, the Registrar is not rigid and uses its discretion in its attempt to censor names with inflated claims, suggesting governmental patronage or duplicating existing ones.

The Registrar of Companies also happens to be the government agency which controls the establishment of new companies and regulates existing ones in terms of the South African Companies Act.

Private or public

Any foreigner who intends to establish a *subsidiary* or an *affiliate* in South Africa, has a choice between *private* or *public companies.* As elsewhere a *public company* in South Africa may offer shares to the public and in terms of local law 't must have at least seven members and file its annual accounts with the Registrar of Companies, where they are available for public inspection.

A *private company,* on the other hand, is not permitted to offer its shares to the public. It can have either one or more members and must restrict transfer of shares to a membership not exceeding fifty.

While a public company must have at least two directors, a private company needs only one. And in the case of a private company its auditor may also serve as the full-time secretary and bookkeeper — provided of course that he is qualified.

Registration

The method of registration for both *private* and *public companies* is basically the same. And once the foreign entrepreneur has obtained the services of a reputable legal firm (attorneys, not advocates) he may as well leave the rest in their hands.

With power-of-attorney such a local firm will proceed by submitting to the Registrar of Companies a Memorandum and Articles of Association. In the Memorandum of Association the applicant outlines the purpose and main business of the proposed company, while in the Articles of Association the internal structure of the company is outlined. It usually contains information concerning share certificates, transfer of shares and voting rights, meetings of directors and shareholders, accounts and borrowing powers of the company as well as the qualifications of its directors.

Once the Registrar of Companies has approved these applications as well as the proposed name of the new company, it will issue a Certificate to Commence Business, entitling the applicant to proceed with his operations. Although a company can only apply for a Certificate to commence business *after* its incorporation by the Registrar of Companies, it has become practice to submit these applications simultaneously in an effort to expedite matters.

Although the cost of establishing a public company can run higher for obvious reasons, the average legal fee for establishing a private company is R500, excluding registration and stamp fees payable to the Registrar. The latter is nominal.

Local involvement
Although it is as prudent in South Africa as in any other country to involve local personalities in foreign subsidiaries, either as directors or shareholders, there is absolutely no legal requirement in this regard. The share capital of a public or private limited company in South Africa may be wholly owned by non-residents without in any way affecting their status as registered *South African* companies. It is only in matters such as borrowing or credit where they may experience some restrictions.

On the other hand, external companies opting to do business in South Africa through a branch instead of a properly incorporated subsidiary or affiliate company, will find themselves subject to a different set of rules.

Branch
There is the understandable tendency on the part of the South African authorities to consider such branch operations as short-term ventures in contrast to the permanent or long-term presence signified by fully incorporated local subsidiaries. A branch of an external company is undoubtedly at a distinct disadvantage when competing for government or semi-government business against such subsidiaries.

Also in taxes and duties the branch operation finds itself in a different category. While it may actually gain somewhat by being exempt from Non-Resident Shareholders Tax, it is bound to lose out on some of the tax deductions allowed to locally incorporated companies and to pay more in annual duty. An external company is liable, for example, to pay duty on its total capital account (even that portion unrelated to the South African operation) while a subsidiary obviously only pays duty in terms of its own and not its parent company's finances.

It is conceivable, however, that some foreign entrepreneurs may still find it preferable in some circumstances to resort to a local branch instead of an incorporated local company to conduct its business with South Africa.

In such a case, the external company must file within twenty-one days after establishing a local branch the following with the Registrar of Companies:

A certified copy of its Memorandum of Association, the name and address of its auditor, a list of its directors, local manager and secretary, and proof of payment of annual duty.

Under special circumstances, the South African authorities have in the past waived these rules for branches of external companies. These were cases where such external companies could actually prove that registration was not in the South African public interest or impracticable or harmful to the overseas company or its members.

Property
Regardless of whether the foreign entrepreneur opts for a fully incorporated local subsidiary or simply a branch, he can rest assured that there is nothing that precludes him from owning fixed property in South Africa.

Anyone who wishes to start up a business in South Africa simply needs to sort out his own priorities and then proceed to any of a number of expert legal firms to do the rest. He can either approach them directly or through commercial banks. In both cases the cost is reasonable.

ESTABLISHING A FACTORY

South Africa promotes itself as a country with an abundance of labour, raw materials and facilities at modest cost to the foreign investor. The returns are all but modest. South Africa offers the foreign investor one of the highest profit margins in the world at an average of 15 to 17%.

Envisaged for the future is a so-called Constellation of States, encompassing South Africa and its neighbours in an economic union of sorts. This enlarged region is promised as a bonanza to all those who wish to establish manufacturing plants in South Africa (See CONSTELLATION OF STATES).

Stability

Those who insist that unrest in and around South Africa makes investment in that country a risky venture, are referred by government spokesmen to several independent overseas assessments. Most of these expert analysts still rate South Africa among the top fifteen world-wide as far as stability is concerned. (See RISK FACTOR).

South Africa likes to remind everyone that in contrast to other countries in Africa and in the developing world, it has never nationalised or expropriated any property or industry.

Finally, South Africa hastens to point out that the foreign investor is treated on a basis of complete equality with home-grown enterprises. This is true in a general sense, but not altogether accurate.

On the one hand, a foreigner is favoured above the local entrepreneur by being allowed to invest in factories in terms of Financial Rand. At the usual discount of around 25% on the Commercial Rand, a plant that would cost the South African industrialist $10 million to acquire or establish, would cost the overseas investor only $7½ million. (See EXCHANGE CONTROL for further detail concerning Financial Rand transactions). On the other hand, the foreign entrepreneur is restricted in terms of local borrowing. (See LOCAL BORROWING).

Red Carpet

In South Africa the foreign investor can definitely count on red carpet treatment. This country more than welcomes foreign capital and know-how. It actively pursues and will go to great lengths to obtain such foreign participation.

Applications for the establishment or expansion of factories in the main industrial areas of South Africa have to be submitted to the Department of Environmental Planning and Energy, Private Bag X213, Pretoria 0001. They will be judged in terms of the Physical Planning and Utilisation of Resources Act. Labour intensive industries are usually encouraged to move to labour surplus areas in and adjacent to the traditional black homelands or national states. Unless the proposed new industry fulfills a particular need in these industrialised areas, is locality bound, or promises the desired labour ratio, chances are that the Department of Planning will redirect the applicant to any of the following institutions: The Decentralisation Board at the Department of Industries, the Industrial Development Corporation or the Corporation for Economic Development. All three are actively engaged in assisting and promoting industrial decentralisation.

Decentralisation

Decentralisation is a policy which has been actively pursued in recent years not only in South Africa but in many other parts of the world. The basic aim is economic — an effort to alleviate pressures on a few urban centres by bringing industry and development to the hinterland or rural areas, instead of allowing uncontrollable masses of people to swarm to the cities in search of work.

In South Africa industrial development has been mostly confined to four urban areas — Pretoria/Witwatersrand/Vereeniging (the PWV complex), the South-Western Cape region, and the areas of Durban/Pinetown, and Uitenhage/Port Elizabeth. These four areas actually account for 80% of South Africa's industrial production, while comprising hardly 3% of the total land area of the country.

Political overtones

But decentralisation in South Africa is not only an economic affair. It also has political overtones. These so-called *economic development areas* outside South Africa's industrial main-stream to which it wishes to divert new industry — both foreign and local — happen to centre around the traditional black homelands. South Africa has already granted independence to several of these black states, and its declared purpose is to make them all sovereign.

Economic self-sufficiency is seen as a prerequisite for political self-rule and in this way the programme of decentralisation actively contributes towards the end-goal: economically viable, independent black states co-existing with the remaining, mostly white, South Africa. (For further details see BLACK STATES POLICY).

New Emphasis

In recent times the emphasis has shifted somewhat from the political to the economic as far as decentralisation is concerned. The South African government has indicated that it no longer considered political boundaries between the black homelands or national states and the remainder of South Africa as vital when it came to regional development outside the existing industrial areas.

The choice

Foreign entrepreneurs who are redirected to decentralisation areas after applying for permission to establish themselves in one of the major industrial areas, seldom complain in the end. Unusual incentives and concessions and an abundance of services and labour make decentralisation in South Africa a lucrative proposition for most investors. (See DECENTRALISATION INCENTIVES).

DECENTRALISATION INCENTIVES

Once a foreign entrepreneur has decided to expand his operations to South Africa, he will be faced with an important choice: Whether to establish his factory in one of South Africa's four major metropolitan centres or to follow others to the so-called economic development areas.

If his proposed factory does not qualify in terms of the Physical Planning and Utilisation of Resources Act for a site within the existing industrial centres, he will not have to make the choice. It is likely that he will be redirected to growth points outside the four major industrial complexes. (See ESTABLISHING A FACTORY).

In the past the South African authorities actively steered especially new labour-intensive industry to the hinterland in and around the black homelands or national states. Nowadays, with a growing awareness abroad of the many advantages and unusual concessions and incentives offered to investors in the decentralised regions, such action had become almost unnecessary. Foreigners are establishing themselves in these economic development areas on their own initiative.

Basic aim

In South Africa as elsewhere in the world where decentralisation is declared policy, the basic aim is to bring industry and development to the hinterland instead of having workseekers flooding the cities in uncontrollable numbers. But decentralisation in South Africa also has its political side. The underdeveloped areas to which the authorities wish to bring industrial growth and development happen to be on the borders of and inside the black homelands. These national states are all destined to follow Transkei, Bophuthatswana, and Venda to independence, but before independence some measure of economic self-sufficiency is considered necessary. Hence the need for decentralisation and industrial development in these regions.

At first economic self-sufficiency within the geographical borders of these individual black homelands was considered vital, but nowadays the emphasis is on regional development instead. No longer are black national states or homelands considered as self-contained units, but rather as part of a larger regional economic development plan. Recent steps included the establishment of a Development Bank for Southern Africa and a privately managed Small Business Development Corporation.

Regulating bodies

While the Department of Planning regulates the establishment of new industries in the four major industrial areas of South Africa — Pretoria/Witwatersrand/Vereeniging (the PWV complex), the Southwestern Cape region, and the areas of Durban/Pinetown, and Uitenhage/Port Elizabeth — expansion into the decentralised area is handled by three bodies:

The Decentralisation Board
Department of Industries
Private Bag X342
Pretoria 0001

The Industrial Development Corporation
P.O. Box 6905
Johannesburg 2000

The Corporation for Economic Development
P.O. Box 213
Pretoria 0001

The Decentralisation Board fulfills an overseeing role, while the Industrial Development Corporation (IDC) is actively engaged assisting in the establishment of new industry on the borders of the black national states. The Corporation for Economic Development, on the other hand, concerns itself with new industry in the black homelands themselves. Also, some of these states have their own development corporations which liaise directly with potential investors, for example, the Ciskeian National Development Corporation. Private Bag X463, King William's Town 5600.

Concessions

Both the IDC and the CED provide extensive concessions and incentives once the Decentralisation Board approves an applicant. These concessions include low interest loans, income tax concessions, railage rebates and price preferences.

Following are some of the concessions currently offered by one of the black states, the Ciskei, through its National Development Corporation:

★ Loan capital at an annual interest rate of 2.8%.

★ Factories built to individual specifications at annual rentals equal to 5.8% of the cost of the land and buildings.

★ Housing loans for key managerial staff.

★ A 40% railage rebate on manufactured goods.

★ 50% harbour dues rebate on goods shipped to any South African port via East London.

★ Up to 10% price preferences on tenders for a range of government purchases.

★ An income tax rebate of 50% of the wages paid to black workers during the first seven years after establishment of a factory; and 30% of the book value of the manufacturing equipment at the rate of 10%

per annum. (These rebates are deductable from actual payable tax).

Participants

Since its inception a few years ago the decentralisation incentives programme has lured a large number of South African and foreign companies to the black states and their borders. Companies from the United States, Britain, Canada, West Germany, France, Switzerland, Italy and the Netherlands are among those represented in more than 250 factories established since the programme started.

Although the accent is on labour intensive industries, several capital intensive ventures have been established as well. Some recent examples: Auto bodyworks, tea, timber, radio and TV manufacturing plants, porcelain and textile industries.

INDUSTRIAL LEGISLATION

Measured by modern international standards, South Africa's business and industrial community is not overregulated. Here are some of the laws which may concern the foreign businessman intending to establish himself in or to trade with South Africa:

The Physical Planning and Utilisation of Resources Act enables the government to decentralise industry towards the black homelands or national states and to regulate the influx of black workers into the existing white metropolitan areas. In terms of this legislation new factories in the major industrial centres may not without prior approval employ any black workers, and existing factories may not employ any additional black workers without such permission by the authorities.

If the South African government seems doctrinaire in respect of siting and employment of black workers in so-called white cities, it appears to be refreshingly relaxed and realistic in other respects. Despite its long-standing conservationist attitude, the government makes no unreasonable or impractical demands on industry in regard to pollution. At the same time its adherence to the free enterprise principle did not lead to stifling anti-trust or anti-monopolistic legislation.

The acts governing these aspects of South African business are:

★ *The Atmospheric Pollution Prevention Act* distinguishes between control of noxious or offensive gases on the one hand and control of atmospheric pollution by smoke on the other. While smoke control is handled by local authorities, the government through its Chief Pollution Control Officer schedules and regulates offensive gases. (See also POLLUTION CONTROL).

★ *The Foodstuffs, Cosmetics and Disinfectants Act* controls the sale, manufacture, and importation of foodstuffs, cosmetics, and disinfectants. It also prohibits false or misleading advertising relating to these products.

★ *The Maintenance and Promotion of Competition Act* provides for maintenance and promotion of competition in the economy, the prevention or control of restrictive practices, and governs the acquisition of controlling interests in businesses and undertakings. Instead of listing prohibitions and malpractices (as in the U.S. Anti-Trust legislation) this Act stipulates that a development can only be declared illegal after proper investigation by the so-called Competition Board.

Apart from these Acts, the following legislation is specifically geared towards consumer protection:

★ *The Trade Practices Act* prohibits all forms of false and misleading advertising and prohibits, for instance, the use of trade coupons to promote sales.

★ *The Price Control Act* authorises the Price Controller to introduce controls where and when it is considered necessary to do so. The Controller is entitled to use any of the following three methods: (a) Prescribing specific maximum selling prices for particular goods or services; (b) prescribing the maximum gross profit margins which distributors may take; and (c) freezing prices at the levels prevailing on a specific date. A full list of goods and services subject to price control in terms of this Act can be obtained from the Price Controller, Department of Commerce and Consumer Affairs, Pretoria.

Mining and prospecting are governed by the following legislation:

★ *The Mines and Works Act* basically concerns the safety, health and welfare of employees and the protection of property and public against possible mining hazards.

★ *The Precious Stones Act* regulates and controls the prospecting, mining and sales of precious stones.

★ *The Mining Rights Act* regulates prospecting and mining for precious metals, base minerals and natural oil.

★ *The Atomic Energy Act* controls prospecting for and mining, processing, possession and disposal of source material containing uranium and thorium.

★ *The Mineral Laws Supplementary Act* limits the extent to which mineral rights can be divided. (See also MINERALS).

Reacting to pressures from abroad by disinvestment and so-called corporate responsibility groups on foreign subsidiaries in South Africa, the government passed *The Protection of Businesses Act.* This legislation prohibits anyone from furnishing information regarding their operations on a directive from abroad or within the country, unless the Minister of Industries, Commerce and Consumer Affairs permits. Also according to this Act, geared to protect business from undue harassment, no directive, foreign judgment or order can be enforced in South Africa without prior permission from this Minister. (See also DISINVESTMENT PRESSURES and LABOUR CODES).

There are a wide range of Acts governing employment, wages, workmen's compensation and social security which will concern the foreign investor once he establishes operations in South Africa. At this stage, however, this legislation is undergoing overhaul in terms of recommendations made by the Riekert and Wiehahn Commissions. (See also LABOUR PRACTICES).

POLLUTION CONTROL

As in other modern industrial countries, pollution control and environmental protection are major concerns in South Africa. Controls have, however, been introduced with restraint in order to avoid unnecessarily stringent measures that would excessively inhibit industry. At the same time much effort goes into research and devising new ways to combat pollution.

The Department of Environmental Planning and Energy has the major responsibility in this area. Permission is given or withheld for the establishment of new factories or the expansion of existing ones in terms of their environmental impact.

The Council for Scientific and Industrial Research (CSIR) in Pretoria co-ordinates environmental research by government bodies and universities. On an average it has a total of close to four hundred separate research projects underway. The South African Bureau of Standards (SABS), also headquartered in Pretoria, assists in devising practical ways to control pollution.

Legislation

Although there is other legislation, such as the Public Health Act, with environmental and anti-pollution implications, the major laws affecting overseas investors are:

Atmospheric Pollution Prevention Act: Any factory emitting gases proscribed by this Act as noxious and offensive, has to satisfy the Chief Air Pollution Control Officer, Private Bag X88, Pretoria, that the "best practicable means" have been employed to control emission *before* it can become legally registered. This Act also empowers local authorities to introduce smoke-control measures for factories operating in their areas.

Foodstuffs, Cosmetics and Disinfectants Act: This legislation controls the sale, manufacture and importation of foodstuffs, cosmetics and disinfectants. It also prohibits false and misleading advertising relating to these items.

Prevention and Combating of Pollution of the Sea by Oil Act: This outlaws the discharge of oil by ships in areas around the South African coast. It entitles, for example, a port captain to prevent a ship from leaving if he has reason to believe that it would spill oil.

Atoms and animals

The Atomic Energy Board (AEB) controls both the use of radioactive materials and the disposal of radioactive waste, while the Fuel Research Institute devises new ways of developing smokeless and pollution-free fuel burning. In charge of overseeing the protection of South Africa's extensive animal and plant life, is the National Parks Board.

LABOUR PRACTICES

Ever since the first contact between white and black in South Africa a few centuries ago, discriminatory labour practices existed. It was customary from the very beginning for the white settler from Europe to perform skilled tasks while leaving unskilled work to the uninitiated black African. In South Africa — as in the United States — the universal gap between skilled and unskilled wages assumed racial overtones.

This wage gap did not discourage black work seekers from migrating to the "white cities" in large numbers. They needed little encouragement to exchange their traditional subsistence existence in the tribal homelands for the bright lights of the cities. At the same time the white man badly needed their help to keep the multiplying machinery of modern society going.

The sustained industrial development after the second world war and particularly the economic boom of the late sixties and early seventies caused the stream of black workseekers to become a flood. Due to a continued shortage of whites to fill posts, many semi-skilled and skilled jobs became available to non-whites. In most cases employers actually paid these blacks less than the going rate for whites. At the same time the almost uncontrollable influx of blacks led to housing shortages and abominable shanty towns around the cities.

Discriminatory legislation

This, in abbreviated and simplistic fashion, is the background to the introduction of several discriminatory labour and other laws by the white authorities. One of these served to strengthen controls on the movement of blacks from their homelands to the white urban areas — so-called influx control. Another reserved certain jobs for whites only — job reservation. Although apprenticeship training for blacks was not prohibited by law, it nevertheless was the policy not to indenture blacks as apprentices in designated trades. The wage gap kept widening to the point where skilled Whites earned seven or eight times as much as the Black unskilled worker. Black trade unions were not recognised — only non-black unions.

Elimination steps

In recent years the South African government has set about in a systematic way to abolish discriminatory legislation and practices. These steps, the authorities insist, are not in response to criticism from abroad but developments and pressures inside. They admit that their efforts are not purely humanitarian or altruistic, but also greatly inspired by self-interest. Elimination of discriminatory practices, they argue, would take the brakes off some industries which were seriously hampered by shortage of manpower as a result of influx control and job reservation. There is also the belief that better paid and organized black workers would contribute largely to higher productivity in the end.

Commission

The *Wiehahn Commission* was appointed in June of 1977 to undertake independent investigations and to recommend changes in existing labour practices. In its first report early in 1979, this Commission urged that discrimination and dualism in the South African system should be abolished. It recommended freedom of association for all races in trade unions, removal of job reservation and barriers to equal training and job mobility, as well as desegregation of facilities for all races at the work place. These recommendations were accepted and are in a process of implementation by the government.

Another government appointed body, the *Riekert Commission* addressed itself more specifically to the elimination of the hardships, handicaps and manpower bottlenecks imposed by the so-called influx control of blacks into white urban areas. Riekert called for far-reaching modifications to make it easier for black workseekers and their families to be accommodated in these areas. It also repudiated any form of job discrimination.

Wage gap

It is evident that as part of the major overhaul of the South African labour system, the question of equal wages features prominently.

The most significant wage gap — and one that is found in all countries and pay structures — is the pay gap between skilled and unskilled workers. In South Africa the problem is aggravated by the fact that unskilled work categories are largely dominated by blacks, while the skilled work categories are dominated by whites. This situation is changing rapidly. Elimination of job reservation, new bargaining power for black trade unions and special education and training programmes for black workers are contributing towards this upward movement. The South African government, in addition to training undertaken by private industry, has opened more than forty training centres for blacks.

Once blacks enter the skilled ranks there are no legal obstacles to equal pay for equal work. The South African authorities, incidentally, have never set any ceiling on wages for either skilled or unskilled black workers — only minimum rates. The *Wiehahn Commission* recommended strict adherence to the principle of equal pay for work of equal value. None of the various employment codes enunciated by Sullivan, the EEC and others, concerning equal pay, are in conflict with South African law or official attitude. (See LABOUR CODES).

Minimum wages

Still, despite all this upward movement of black workers into the skilled ranks, it is reasonable to expect that for some time still blacks will continue to perform most of the unskilled and semi-skilled work in South

Africa. It is the intention of all — government and employers and trade unions — to remove the seven or eight to one discrepancy between skilled and unskilled wages. The fact that unskilled jobs are mostly held by blacks and skilled positions by whites, gave this argument a racial colouring. Others have argued, somewhat more realistically, that unskilled wages should be improved for their own sake — not merely in response to an imbalance with skilled wages, but to make it possible for the average workers to maintain a reasonable living standard.

The problem remains one of finding a universally acceptable minimum wage level. A good measure of the extent of the disagreement in this area is the proliferation of terms such as Minimum Living Level (MLL), Poverty Datum Line (PDL), Minimum Subsistence Level (MSL) and Household Subsistence Level (HSL) — all purporting to signify the ultimate yardstick for minimum wages in different ways.

Nevertheless there is a markable shift in the relationship between black and white wages — a determined effort to narrow the wage gap. In the past five years, for example, the average *real* wage for blacks increased at an annual rate of 8 percent, while the figure for whites was 1.3 percent.

Cheap labour
The purpose of this brief overview of South Africa's changing labour scene is in part aimed at cautioning those few abroad who may still be under the mistaken impression that good profits can be made out there by paying exceptionally low wages. Anyone who expects to find cheap labour in South Africa should think twice before moving machinery and capital to that country. It may have been, but it is rapidly becoming something of the past. On the other hand foreign entrepreneurs may still find the overall wage structure in South Africa low in comparison with that of their own country. Also, once they have investigated other incentives and concessions, they may discover that the production cost is low *despite* rising wages in South Africa. (See TAXES, ESTABLISHING A FACTORY and DECENTRALISATION INCENTIVES).

An important footnote: With more than 250,000 new workers entering the South African labour market each year, there is hardly any need for concern about the availability of workers.

Chapter 6

TRADE

EXPORTS/IMPORTS

An exporter of raw materials and importer of manufactured goods. This is how South Africa is perceived by many. This view is erroneous.

While South Africa still relies heavily on the sales of gold and other minerals as well as agricultural products, it also has developed into a formidable exporter of manufactured goods. Sales of manufactured goods already equal that of gold.

Sophisticated

South Africa has a sophisticated industrial base, developed around a thriving mining industry. It produces its own jet aircraft and motor vehicles, electronic goods and heavy engineering equipment as well as chemicals. It has grown into a major supplier of phosphoric acid to the world. The cost of production in most cases is such that South Africa can afford to compete successfully abroad. (See MANUFACTURING INDUSTRY). South Africans point proudly to sales of their mufflers to Detroit and mining machinery to almost every part of the world as examples of this competitiveness.

Exporting to SA

It would therefore be naive to assume that South Africa stands ready to buy anything sophisticated from abroad. Some potential exporters may indeed find that instead of wanting their manufactures, South Africa wishes to sell the same to them at a much lower price.

Still, detailed import statistics for the seventies indicate that South Africa remains in need of much in the way of manufactured goods — especially capital goods and equipment for its growing manufacturing industry:

Business makes the world go round. Bonuskor means business.

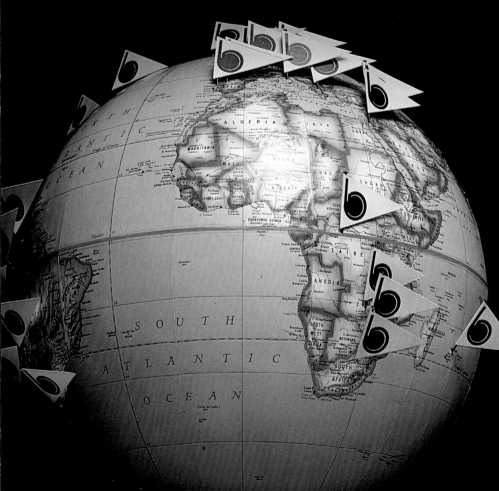

Bonuskor is a giant export/import corporation in South Africa. We trade with 42 countries. Competing with some of the most sophisticated local products in the world. Successfully. Because we mean business.

We refuse to get stalled by red tape. So if you're looking for a South African trade link, Bonuskor is your contact. Specialities of the group are agriculture, forestry, special steels, machine tools, motorcycles, white goods, industrial engines, pumps, generators, instrumentation cables, control valves, gauging instruments, or any of the related industries.

Your best call is Bonuskor. Talk to us first. We mean business. Bonuskor. PO Box 61340, Marshalltown 2107. Republic of South Africa. Tel No: 836-0721.

BONUSKOR

Sections	R-million							
	1971	1972	1973	1974*	1975*	1976	1977	1978
Live animals; animal products	36,0	25,2	38,5	60,5	53,4	40,6	32,0	24,6
Vegetable products	54,6	53,2	75,2	101,0	106,0	121,9	176,4	144,0
Animal and vegetable fats and oils and their cleavage products; prepared edible fats; animal and vegetable waxes	15,2	14,3	25,6	40,6	26,8	40,5	41,6	41,2
Prepared foodstuffs; beverages, spirits and vinegar; tobacco	48,0	44,5	57,7	84,4	110,1	105,8	99,2	116,0
Mineral products	23,5	33,2	38,6	95,7	76,4	106,1	106,3	114,8
Products of the chemical and allied industries	186,6	198,6	257,3	448,3	450,6	486,7	506,7	652,3
Artificial resins and plastic materials, cellulose esters and ethers and articles thereof; rubber, synthetic rubber, factice and articles thereof	102,3	96,6	139,1	278,0	199,2	247,0	219,1	265,3
Raw hides and skins, leather, fur, skins and articles thereof; saddlery and harness; travel goods, handbags and the like; articles of gut (other than silk-worm gut)	15,1	17,4	19,6	23,6	22,0	31,7	22,5	25,6
Wood and articles of wood; wood charcoal; cork and articles of cork; manufactures of straw, of esparto and of other plaiting materials; basketware and wickerwork	30,6	28,3	52,3	63,8	54,4	55,0	34,7	45,1
Paper-making material; paper and paper-board and articles thereof	85,5	87,4	117,8	203,7	158,8	175,5	163,3	184,6
Textiles and textile articles	257,8	249,9	326,7	464,9	334,1	430,4	325,0	365,0
Footwear, headgear, umbrellas, sunshades, whips, riding-crops and parts thereof; prepared feathers and articles made therewith; artificial flowers; articles of human hair; fans	16,0	14,6	18,5	23,9	28,4	33,0	25,9	30,9
Articles of stone, plaster, cement, asbestos, mica and similar materials; ceramic products; glass and glassware	33,3	32,9	45,8	61,0	68,6	69,3	55,9	72,7
Pearls, precious and semi-precious stones, precious metals, rolled precious metals, and articles thereof; imitation jewellery; coinage	17,7	24,6	32,1	42,9	67,3	56,2	50,1	29,4
Base metals and articles of base metal	235,5	161,7	244,3	507,9	567,6	360,6	322,1	364,7
Machinery and mechanical appliances; electrical equipment and parts thereof	785,1	772,9	977,6	1 320,6	1 819,4	1 937,4	1 642,7	2 108,7
Vehicles, aircraft and parts thereof; vessels and certain associated transport equipment	579,7	569,7	601,5	789,4	1 083,9	1 235,3	996,0	1 350,7
Optical photographic, cinematographic, measuring, checking, precision, medical and surgical instruments and apparatus; clocks and watches; musical instruments; sound recorders and reproducers and parts thereof	97,9	106,5	129,3	179,4	205,8	209,7	204,7	243,8
Miscellaneous manufactured articles	25,4	22,3	31,4	42,1	44,2	45,6	42,9	48,8
TOTAL	2 698,7	2 628,6	3 282,2	4 898,0	5 545,0	5 859,4	5 118,3	6 262,5

* Preliminary figures

Works of art, collector's pieces and antiques as well as other unclassified goods excluded.

Source: Department of Customs and Excise.

Import controls

South Africa subscribes to the General Agreement on Tariffs and Trade. Import controls are therefore within the framework of GATT. It is administered by the Director of Import and Export of the Department of Commerce and Consumer Affairs.

Before investing in any venture involving the importation into South Africa of plant, machinery, raw materials or other goods, the foreign entrepreneur should acquaint himself with the relevant regulations. Normally the authorities distinguish between the following three categories of imports:

(1) Goods that may be imported without an import permit (Free list).

(2) Goods in respect of which permits will be granted to meet the full reasonable requirements of importers. This category includes, generally, industrial plant and machinery, equipment, spares, accessories, raw materials and consumable stores as well as those consumer commodities for which import quotas were previously granted.

(3) Goods which are subject to import permits in which the exact nature, volume and value of the imported goods are specified.

Foreigners who had already received approval for the establishment of an industry in South Africa can expect to receive import permits to cover all reasonable requirements, with the exception of goods subject to specific permits.

Further detail concerning import controls can be obtained from South Africa's trade representatives at embassies abroad or directly from the Director of Imports and Exports at the Department of Commerce and Consumer Affairs, Private Bag X84, Pretoria 0001. (Telex: 3667 SA) (Telephone 48-5500).

Customs and excise

The Department of Customs and Excise bases its tariffs for imported goods on the international Customs Co-operation Council Nomenclature (CCCN). Rebates of customs duty are allowed on certain goods imported for manufacturing purposes, while duties may be imposed on others in order to protect local industry. Details are obtainable directly from this Department or South Africa's trade representatives abroad:
Department of Customs and Excise
Frans du Toit Building
Private Bag X47
Pretoria 0001.

Importing from SA

Although there is a growing demand abroad for manufactured goods from South Africa, most foreign buying is still in the areas of minerals and agricultural products. (South Africa is the Western world's most important supplier of strategic minerals and among the first six in agricultural sales — See also MINERALS and AGRICULTURE).

Following is an overview of South Africa's exports during the seventies:

Sections	R-million							
	1971	1972	1973	1974*	1975*	1976*	1977*	1978*
Live animals; animal products	43,0	67,2	80,2	54,1	70,5	104,5	156,2	162,6
Vegetable products	170,6	276,2	232,5	403,1	543,1	443,7	427,0	563,3
Animal and vegetable fats and oils and their cleavage products; prepared edible fats; animal and vegetable waxes	8,8	8,7	12,6	40,6	22,7	19,7	29,6	62,2
Prepared foodstuffs; beverages, spirits and vinegar; tobacco	168,4	266,6	275,8	446,6	523,9	503,2	516,6	507,6
Mineral products	175,3	168,0	212,5	286,2	388,1	618,4	881,7	994,7
Products of the chemical and allied industries	63,4	71,4	86,9	116,0	130,5	154,9	231,0	303,4
Artificial resins and plastic materials, cellulose esters and ethers and articles thereof; rubber, synthetic rubber, factice and articles thereof	12,3	14,0	15,6	21,5	18,5	24,2	30,5	37,7
Raw hides and skins, leather, fur skins and articles thereof; saddlery and harness; travel goods, handbags and the like; articles of gut (other than silk-worm gut)	36,6	58,8	73,4	55,3	49,2	82,5	106,0	136,9
Wood and articles of wood; wood charcoal; cork and articles of cork; manufacturers of straw, of esparto and of other plaiting materials; basketware and wickerwork	2,1	2,8	4,3	5,8	4,4	16,0	24,7	33,2
Paper-making material; paper and paperboard and articles thereof	41,7	49,8	66,6	96,1	83,7	95,4	119,5	125,0
Textiles and textile articles	72,7	144,6	206,1	152,3	161,9	232,8	274,5	292,1
Footwear, headgear, umbrellas, sunshades, whips, riding-crops and parts thereof; prepared feathers and articles made therewith; artificial flowers; articles of human hair; fans	1,0	1,2	1,3	1,6	1,5	3,1	6,1	8,2
Articles of stone, plaster, cement, asbestos, mica and similar materials; ceramic products; glass and glassware	8,6	10,3	10,8	14,2	14,1	16,2	23,3	32,8
Pearls, precious and semi-precious stones, precious metals, rolled precious metals, and articles thereof; imitation jewellery; coinage	226,9	316,1	478,7	710,5	994,8	886,9	1 375,0	2 003,2
Base metals and articles of base metal	222,1	289,2	362,4	488,8	485,6	794,4	1 032,2	1 239,1
Machinery and mechanical appliances; electrical equipment and parts thereof	97,5	96,6	106,4	129,3	143,2	150,7	200,1	172,1
Vehicles, aircraft, and parts thereof; vessels and certain associated transport equipment	35,1	36,4	32,8	45,3	51,5	60,6	90,6	107,5
Optical, photographic, cinematographic, measuring, checking, precision, medical and surgical instruments and apparatus; clocks and watches; musical instruments; sound recorders and reproducers and parts thereof	7,7	9,0	9,6	11,1	14,0	17,4	17,1	17,6
TOTAL	1 500,6	1 979,4	2 417,7	3 339,5	3 983,2	4 532,0	5 863,2	7 199,2

* Preliminary figures
Excluding miscellaneous manufactured articles, works of art, etc. and other unclassified goods.
Source: Department of Customs and Excise.

Major customers towards the close of the seventies were the Common Market countries (excluding Britain) at 23.0%, the United States (18.7%), Britain (17.4%) and Japan (10.4%). Africa accounted for 7.4% of total sales abroad. In all, South Africa exports to 125 countries and rates in volume between fifteenth and twentieth among the world's trading nations.

From the winelands of the Cape, where every year is a good year for wine.

The Cape. With its tradition of excellent wines dating back to the eighteenth century and the famous wines of Groot Constantia.

This is also where the word "vintage" takes on a slightly different meaning. For unlike their European counterparts the South African wine regions are blessed with a settled climate which makes every year a good year for wine.

At KWV we add to this gift of nature the expertise gleaned through dedication, research and working in close co-operation with experts from all over the world.

This is why the name KWV is your guarantee of the finest in natural wines, ports, sherries, dessert wines, brandies and liqueurs.

Trade enquiries:
Marketing Manager (International)
KWV P.O. Box 528 Suider-Paarl.
Republic of South Africa Tel: Paarl 22011

KWV

Guardians of a great tradition

Export assistance

Extensive export assistance is available to South African-based industry from government and private bodies. A special Export Promotion Division of the Department of Commerce and Consumer Affairs provides free advice and services to South African exporters through its local offices and representatives abroad. This Department also arranges tax and other special incentives for industries wishing to promote their sales abroad.

The South African Foreign Trade Organization (SAFTO) operates a non-profit export promotion service for a private membership of some nine hundred. SAFTO is active in seventy countries where its representatives regularly visit, but it has permanent offices only in South Africa's major cities. It also assists foreign entrepreneurs to establish export-oriented operations in South Africa:

SAFTO
P.O. Box 9039
Johannesburg 2000
Telex: 960 87269
Telephone: 724 1631

Insurance and Cover

South African exporters can obtain credit insurance for short-, medium-, and long-term transactions from Credit Guarantee Insurance Corporation of Africa Ltd. (CGIC) — a private organisation owned jointly by a number of leading South African banks, financial institutions and insurance companies:

CGIC
Carlton Centre
P.O. Box 9244
Johannesburg 2000.

The S.A. Reserve Bank provides forward foreign exchange cover to South African exporters and importers. Through authorised dealers in foreign exchange the Reserve Bank provides US Dollar/Rand forward cover at a premium over the spot US Dollar/Rand rates of 1% per annum. Where customers require forward cover in currencies other than the US Dollar the foreign currency is covered on the European markets against the US Dollar and the US Dollar/Rand leg of the transaction in turn covered through the Reserve Bank.

Multi-nationals

It has become popular practice among multi-national companies to use their South African subsidiary operation as an export base not only for adjoining African territories but also other world markets. Lower production cost coupled with export incentives enable them to be more competitive this way instead of relying on home-based plants.

CHAMBERS OF COMMERCE

Private enterprise in South Africa is well organised on the basis of the Chambers of Commerce. Existing side by side are the Association of Chambers of Commerce and the Afrikaanse Handelsinstituut. (AHI) (literally Afrikaans Trading Institute). Both these organisations have voluntary membership in the private sector and branches of chapters across the country. They serve as spokesmen for their membership on a variety of official and semi-official bodies. The Association of Chambers of Commerce (ASSOCOM) also acts as the secretariat for the S.A. Council of the International Chamber of Commerce. Both the AHI and ASSOCOM are equipped to assist foreign entrepreneurs with information concerning the South African private sector:

The Afrikaanse Handelsinstituut
P.O. Box 1741
Pretoria
Tel: 21-8311

The Associated Chambers of Commerce
P.O. Box 91267
Auckland Park
Johannesburg
Tel: 726-5300

International chambers

The foreign executive is bound, however, to find in South Africa a Chamber specifically geared to promoting trade and business links between his own country and the Republic of South Africa. These international chambers collect data of particular interest to their membership and are useful specialised sources:

S.A. American Chamber of Commerce
P.O. Box 62280
Marshalltown 2107
Johannesburg
Tel: 834 7581

S.A. Belgian Chamber of Commerce
P.O. Box 70390
Bryanston 2021
Johannesburg
Tel: 706 1219

S.A. French Chamber of Commerce
P.O. Box 61064
Marshalltown 2107
Johannesburg
Tel: 836 6677

Principal Cities

Johannesburg

Cape Town

Entrance to the Houses of Parliament, Cape Town

Durban

Pretoria

S.A. German Chamber of Trade and Industry
P.O. Box 91004
Auckland Park 2006
Johannesburg
Tel: 726 7200

S.A. Israeli Chamber of Economic Relations
P.O. Box 694
Johannesburg 2000
Tel: 726 5309

S.A. British Trade Association
P.O. Box 10329
Johannesburg
Tel: 838 4784

S.A. South American Chamber of Economic Relations
P.O. Box 694
Johannesburg 2000
Tel: 726 5309

S.A. Taiwan Chamber of Commerce
P.O. Box 694
Johannesburg 2000
Tel: 726 5309

Wine Estate

Pictures:
S.A. Panorama

Union Buildings,
Pretoria

PATENTS, TRADEMARKS AND COPYRIGHT

Patents

Patent law in South Africa is based on British law. South Africa belongs to the Paris Union Convention for the Protection of Industrial Property and it enjoys full reciprocal rights with other treaty members. To be patentable, an invention must relate to a new and useful art, process, machine, manufacture or composition of matter. Application for patent protection has to be filed in the·usual fashion through a patent attorney in South Africa. The Patent Office will not consider applications directly from foreign persons or foreign patent attorneys. The term of a patent is sixteen years, but application may be made to extend the term on the grounds of inadequate rewards from the use of the patent.

Trademarks and designs

Trademarks relating to goods or services which are inherently distinctive or capable of becoming distinctive may be registered by local or foreign enterprises in South Africa. Registration is for an initial term of ten years, renewable for further ten year periods.

Copyright

Protection is given in South Africa to literary, dramatic, musical and artistic works, sound recordings, cinematographic films, broadcasts and published editions of works originating in South Africa, or in countries which are members of the Berne Convention, or by special arrangement in the United States. Where publication first takes place in a country, other than the U.S., or which is not a member of the Berne Convention, protection can be obtained in South Africa through simultaneous publication in a Berne Convention country.

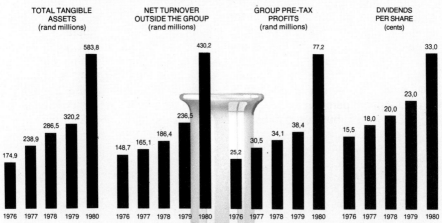
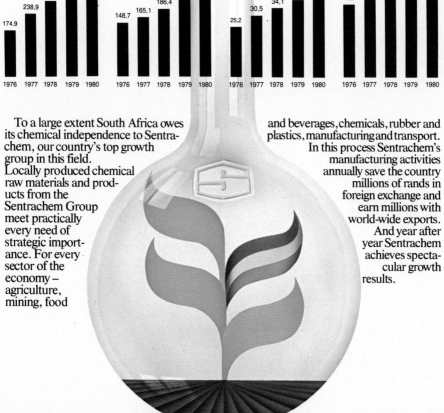

CONSUMER MARKET

Although white South Africans are in the minority their total income outstrips that of other races. Their standard of living and taste corresponds to that of developed Western Europe and America. At the moment, therefore, those who market sophisticated, and especially luxury goods, are generally inclined to target themselves on this white population group.

A shift is imminent as blacks enter the skilled ranks in increasing numbers and the wage gap narrows. Newly introduced labour practices will serve to speed this process further. (See LABOUR PRACTICES).

Statistics

This is how the Pretoria-based Bureau of Market Research recorded the narrowing per capita income gap between the different major population groups of South Africa. It based its *real* per capita income figures on 1974/1975 prices:

Year		1959/60	1964/65	1969/70	1974/75	1980
Whites	R	1724	2 041	2 487	2 584	2 744
Blacks	R	154	160	200	235	305
Coloureds	R	274	329	412	516	631
Asians	R	309	393	499	583	748

Figures compiled with the aid of the Department of Statistics and private sources support the following diminishing ratio between white and other races as far as the wage gap is concerned:

Monetary Terms	1970	1975	1977	1978
White : Coloured	3,5:1	3,1:1	3,1:1	3,1:1
White : Asian	3,1:1	2,6:1	2,4:1	2,3:1
White : Black	6,8:1	4,9:1	4,4:1	4,3:1

It is also apparent that the continued higher growth rate among blacks will make this market increasingly important not only in numerical terms but in total disposable income. This is how the experts see the growth of South Africa's different groups up to 2020:

	Total	Blacks	Whites	Coloureds	Asians
1970 Census*	22 487 000	15 927 000	3 840 000	2 078 000	642 000
Mid '78 estimate*	27 364 000	19 649 000	4 428 000	2 509 000	778 000
2000 estimate§	50 288 000ß	37 293 000	6 890 000 ß	4 890 000	1 215 000
2020 estimate§	81 339 000ß	62 798 000	9 204 000 ß	7 720 000	1 617 000

* Source: Bureau of Market Research, Pretoria, Research Report No. 73 — includes the de facto populations of Transkei and Bophuthatswana.

§ Source: J. L. Sadie "Projections of South African population 1970-2020".

ß These figures include white immigration of 30 000 per annum.

Multi-market

It goes without saying that any entrepreneur who wishes to do business with all sectors of the South African population needs to make adjustments. While maintaining the same quality and standards in product, it still behooves him to take note of ethnic and racial differences in taste and taboos.

Too often the same businessmen who would never make the mistake of trying to mass-market pork in a Jewish neighbourhood, seem to be blissfully unaware of the customs and beliefs that permeate almost every facet not only of rural black life, but also the ways of the urban black, despite his more Westernised appearance.

Here, in brief, are the main groups and some of their more notable characteristics:

Whites

Totalling four and a half million. Comparable to peoples of advanced Western countries of Europe and America in standard of living and level of sophistication. Two main subgroups: Afrikaners — descendants of mostly Dutch, German and French; and English-speaking — with mostly British ancestry. No need to differentiate between two groups when it comes to products and marketing. Take note, however, that all advertising directed at Afrikaners should be in *good* Afrikaans. The shortest route to offending this group (they form 63 percent of the whites and run the government as well as a lot of businesses) is to ignore or mutilate their language, which is a derivative of Dutch.

Coloureds

At two and a half million this group resides mostly in the Western Cape area. They emulate the whites with whom they have more in common than languages. More than eighty percent speak Afrikaans and the rest English. Basically the Coloureds are what their name implies: people of a mixed or mulatto origin. Among their ancestors are some of the original slaves imported from the Far East, aborigines (Hottentot and Bushmen), Whites and Malays — also some black infusion occurred more recently.

Asians

Three-quarter million. Descended from indentured labour brought from India in the 1860's to work in the sugar cane fields — as well as Indian traders who came independently at the same time. Thirty percent still speak one or more of the Indian vernacular languages such as Tamil, Hindi, Gujarati, Urdu or Telegu. Nevertheless, almost everyone speaks English as well. Although some — especially Moslems — still cling to old customs, their habits have Westernised considerably over the years. Despite introducing to South Africa with success their own traditional hot curry dishes there is the tendency among them to prefer Western dishes themselves. After the whites, the most affluent group. They have long since exchanged the sugar cane fields for positions in commerce, finance and manufacturing and only a few remained in their original jobs.

The Chinese community numbers only 9 000, some of whom date from the days when labour was imported for the gold mines from the Far East early this century. Others are more recent immigrants. Mostly in cities as shopkeepers, restaurant owners and the like.

Blacks

Totalling twenty million. Mistake is often made to group them together as one people. Ever since their arrival in South Africa in the mid-eighteenth century as migrants from the north, the black peoples were sharply divided. Belonging to vastly different nations such as the Zulu, Xhosa, Venda and Sotho they were actually engaged in severe internecine wars at the time when white and black first met. Although the wars are something of the past — and the animosity in most cases — the cultural, linguistic and other differences remained. Especially in dealing with the so-called rural black, the businessman is well advised to take note of these differences. Even in the cities where the process of Westernisation sets in, traditional differences may be buried but often come to the fore when least expected.

Rural blacks

These are black peoples who still basically reside in the lands of their ancestors — the so-called black national states, some of which are already independent. For example, Transkei, Bophuthatswana and Venda. Most of them still buy at trading posts where they display great care and price and quality consciousness in selecting products. Relying to a large measure on subsistence farming, these rural black peoples obviously are interested in the essentials. Still, long before cash remittances from their relatives in the cities started enabling them to move into non-essential buying, they have been buyers of battery operated radios, which also happen to be the best medium after word-of-mouth to reach them with advertising. Radio reaches deep into the rural homelands with services in the vernacular. For the moment television is of no significance to these people. Important to remember is the fact that despite growing literacy in the rural areas, there are still a vast number of older people who cannot read or write and whose buying habits are therefore influenced by packaging, colour and brand-markings.

Urban blacks

Urbanisation of the blacks is happening still at a steady pace despite con-certed efforts by the authorities to stem the tide. (See BLACK STATES POLICY and DECENTRALISATION INCENTIVES). Emerging from a polygamous society, the urban black becomes monogamous and as he moves into the middle class bracket, conscious of the need for family planning. But Western urban influences do not supplant all his beliefs and customs. Although many city dwellers may decry *lobola* and witchcraft, these and other traditional practices remain prevalent. *(Lobola* requires that the groom pays the father of the bride in terms of livestock or cash). Businessmen should never be fooled by appearances in dress and living habits among urban blacks into believing that they are dealing with just another regular Western consumer. Most urban blacks may speak English — the major "black" urban newspapers are in fact in English — and dress in the way of the whites, but they remain true to much of their past beliefs and taboos. Research into these are of utmost importance before tackling the market. Incidentally, some 80 percent of South Africa's urban black population is below the age of fifty — a youth market indeed.

Market information

Detailed information about market characteristics and trends is available from a variety of government, semi-government and private institutions — as well as research institutes run by university business schools.

Here are some sources:

Department of Statistics Steyn's Building 270 Schoeman Street Private Bag X44 Pretoria 0001.	All official figures can be obtained from this source in printed form at reasonable prices.
Bureau of Economic Research University of Stellenbosch Stellenbosch.	Undertakes regular studies of market trends and developments.
Bureau for Economic Research: Co-operation and Development, Poynton Building Pretoria.	BENSO, as it is known undertakes research especially in homelands — government sponsored.
Bureau of Market Research University of South Africa Pretoria.	Non-profit organisation which undertakes extensive market research and publishes its reports for use by industry.

BUSINESS NEWS

How does the foreigner stay on top of financial and business news in South Africa?

Especially since the gold boom of the late seventies the international media are devoting more space to economic developments in South Africa. Still, no foreign executive can keep abreast of events in South Africa by simply consulting the financial pages of his own newspaper or by reading international business publications.

Assuming that this executive does not have an office or operation in South Africa, in which case the accurate flow of information becomes easy, the following sources may be useful:

S.A. Reserve Bank Publications: The central bank publishes Quarterly Bulletins and an Annual Economic Report available by airmail at an annual fee of R25. These authoritative updates are available from The Head, Economics Department, S.A. Reserve Bank, P.O. Box 427, Pretoria 0001.

Perspectives: Produced and distributed very selectively to financial institutions abroad by the South Africa Department of Finance, Private Bag X115, Pretoria 0001.

CM: A monthly newsletter surveying gold and other mining activity from the vantage point of the industry's central body — the South African Chamber of Mines, P.O. Box 809, Johannesburg 2000.

Johannesburg Stock Exchange: Anyone who wishes to keep informed about South African stocks and shares can obtain at reasonable cost from the Johannesburg Stock Exchange, P.O. Box 1174, Johannesburg 2000, an annual two-volume handbook as well as regular monthly updates on all trading.

Government publications: Most South African Embassies abroad publish newsletters and special ad hoc brochures on current political and economic developments. Also available free of charge is S.A. DIGEST, a bi-weekly summary of news and events, from the Department of Foreign Affairs and Information, Private Bag X152, Pretoria.

South Africa: Target or Opportunity: A comparative overview of South Africa compiled by Dr. Jan S. Marais for overseas readers.

Newspapers and Magazines: All South Africa's major newspapers and several financial magazines provide extensive coverage of the local business scene. Some are available by airmail overseas.

METRIC SYSTEM

As a former British possession South Africa used to be tuned to the world in terms of imperial monies, weights and measures. In recent years the Rand replaced the Pound Sterling and the metric system was introduced to measure weight, volume and distance.

Here, for the uninitiated, are a few pointers:

Length:		
1 metre	1.093 yards	3.280 84 feet
Distance:		
1 kilometre	0.538 957 International Nautical miles	0.621 371 miles
Area:		
1 sq. metre	1.195 99 sq. yds.	10.763 9 sq. ft.
Volume:		
1 millilitre	0.035 195 1 fl. oz.	0.061 023 7 cub. inch
1 litre	0.219 969 Imp. gallons	0.035 214 7 cub. ft.
1 cub. metre	1.307 95 cub. yds.	264.172 U.S. gallons 219 969 Imp. gallons
Weights:		
1 gram	5 metric carats	0.035 274 0 ounces
1 kilogram	2.204 62 pounds	

Chapter 7

GOLD, DIAMONDS, AND SHARES

KRUGERRAND

Many refer to South Africa as the country of the Krugerrand. This is hardly surprising. At the close of the seventies this gold coin accounted for ten percent of South Africa's total exports, including the sales of gold bullion.

Performance

This is how the Krugerrand has performed in terms of number sold and total value of sales — in comparison with gold bullion — since marketing started in 1970:

	Krugerrand sales	Krugerrand revenue R'000 000	Bullion revenue R'000 000	Total revenue R'000 000
1970	211 016	8,6	824,6	831,2
1971	550 200	16,6	882,4	899,0
1972	543 700	24,6	1 135,3	1 159,9
1973	859 300	53,8	1 735,5	1 789,3
1974	3 203 675	362,6	2 257,2	2 619,8
1975	4 803 925	589,3	1 971,1	2 560,4
1976	3 004 945	342,9	2 037,3	2 380,2
1977	3 331 344	451,2	2 363,8	2 815,0
1978	6 012 293	1 044,6	2 818,4	3 863,0
1979	4 940 755	1 330,3	4 456,9	5 787,2

Although the number of Krugerrands sold dropped considerably from 1978 to 1979, the total revenue from sales still shows a healthy increase as a result of the rise in the price of gold.

Krugerrand afficionados insist that it pays better to buy the coin instead of simply investing in gold bullion or shares.

Sales are mostly abroad. In South Africa the authorities have strict rationing in force — only 4 000 Krugerrands are released for local purchasing every week. The purpose is not to make individual South Africans into gold hoarders, but to earn foreign exchange by selling to individuals abroad.

Still this starvation diet on Krugerrands in the country of its origin tends to detract from the claim that the coin is legal tender. Russia has taken even a harder line on its golden Chervonets. Its own people are prohibited by law from possessing any.

Competition
The Krugerrand did not become the world's most popular gold coin through lack of competition. Long before it was introduced by the South African Chamber of Mines other countries have placed gold coins in distribution. The Krugerrand is not South Africa's first attempt either. It already had the smaller and less familiar R1 and R2 gold coins, when the idea came up to mint a coin with exactly one ounce in gold content.

Krugerrand was the second choice as far as name is concerned. First choice was Trojan — after Troy ounce — and it would have gone through had the South Africans not discovered at the last moment that Trojan also happened to be the name of a contraceptive widely sold in the United States. President Paul Kruger was the President of the old Transvaal Republic and his face appears on one side of the coin, while the other depicts a local antelope, the Springbok.

If the South African authorities displayed some sloppy research in naming its coin Trojan, other aspects showed meticulous respect for detail. Attention was even given to "stackability" — the rim of a coin determines whether it stacks easily in banks or the vaults of the wealthy. The ordinary buyers who can afford only a few obviously don't care. Earlier this century the United States, however, had to withdraw a very attractive $20 gold piece because it would not stack properly at banks.

To a large extent the Krugerrand first captured the market because it took the guessing out of gold coin values. It was the first of its kind to come in one ounce units each and as such **ordinary** Krugerrands are worth at any given moment the price of gold per ounce plus a premium ranging from 4 to 8 per cent. **Proof** Krugerrands have as collector's items a price structure all their own.

In distribution when the Krugerrand first made its bid for the overseas market were the British gold sovereign and Russian Chervonet (each a quarter ounce in gold content) and a variety of others from Switzerland, Austria and so forth. The Mexican gold peso series in denominations that are difficult to relate to the going price of gold, still managed to capture a fair percentage of especially the U.S. market. (Examples: 50 peso — 1.2057 oz; 20 peso — 0.482 oz; 2 peso — 0.048 oz)

Following the South African example Canada also entered the world market with its one ounce gold Maple Leaf coin. In contrast to the Krugerrand, however, it is made of pure unalloyed gold and therefore somewhat prone to nicks and scratches.

Finally the United States Treasury, despite its long-standing opposition to gold and the Krugerrand, followed suit in 1980 with the one ounce Grant Wood and half ounce Marian Anderson medallions.

Smaller coins
When the one ounce Krugerrand was first introduced to the world market, it enabled the small investor to build up his own bullion reserve at affordable prices per unit. With the meteoric rise in price over the past decade, the one ounce coin had become too expensive for the so-called "man in the street" — Krugerrand's favourite target. South Africa therefore proceeded to mint and market early in the eighties half, quarter and one-tenth ounce Krugerrands.

Marketing
Marketing of the Krugerrand series is handled exclusively from South Africa by the S.A. Chamber of Mines through its International Gold Corporation — INTERGOLD. The coins are primarily sold through an overseas distribution network consisting of fourteen major banks and bullion dealers:

Germany
Bayerische Landesbank
Deutsche Bank AG

Switzerland
Swiss Bank Corporation
Swiss Credit Bank
Union Bank of Switzerland

United States
J. Aron & Company Inc.
Mocatta Metals Corporation
Republic National Bank of New York

United Kingdom
Johnson Matthey (Bankers) Ltd.
Mocatta and Goldsmid Ltd.
Samuel Montagne & Co. Ltd.
N.M. Rothschild & Sons Ltd.
Sharps Pixley Ltd.

Canada
Bank of Novia Scotia

Method of marketing varies of course from one country to another. In Germany, for instance, the two prime distributors — Deutsche Bank and Bayerische Landesbank — simply sell the coins at each of their 17 500 branches. In the United States, however, the system is more complicated due to the absence of a nationwide banking system. Also when Krugerrands were first introduced the U.S. Treasury actively discouraged banks from getting involved. Sales are mostly handled by way of coin dealers, stockbroking channels, investment consultants and precious metal direct response firms, the latter on a mail order basis.

Proof Krugers
Untouched by human hands. That is the way of proof Krugerrands, which are literally handled with gloves only. After proper individual examination under a magnifying glass to ensure perfection, these coins are packaged in plastic containers and shipped — one per person — to twelve thousand proof coin dealers on the list of the S.A. Mint. Detail on how to obtain these precious coins is available from the South African Mint, 103 Visagie Street, P.O. Box 464, Pretoria.

DIAMONDS

The first diamond was discovered in South Africa in 1866. It soon became the world's major producer of gem diamonds — a position it held ever since. South Africa has its own diamond cutting industry, geared basically to the processing of diamonds of one carat and over.

In recent times diamonds have apart from jewellery items and female adornments become hard asset investments — a hedge against inflation. According to available statistics R10 000 invested in 1971 at 10% compound interest per annum in bank deposits, buildings society shares, mortgage bonds or government stock, would in 1980 have amounted to R23 579. The same R10 000 invested in flawless blue white diamonds in 1971 would have been worth R275 478.

The following chart provides a comparative picture between diamonds and other forms of investment:

	Cost of single item in:				Value of an investment of R10 000 made in 1971:			
	1971	1974	1978	1980	1971	1974	1978	1980
	R	R	R	R	R	R	R	R
GOLD Ordinary (uncirculated) Krugerrands	34	150	180	510	10 000	44 100	52 920	149 940
DIAMONDS 1ct Flawless Blue White	1 360	3 748	7 720	37 480	10 000	27 547	56 742	275 478
STAMPS Mint SA One Pound — 1916	150	240	1 000	2 000	10 000	15 984	66 600	133 200
RARE COINS 1926 South African Farthing	1 200	7 500	10 600	14 000	10 000	62 250	87 980	116 200
PERSIAN RUGS Rashtidazeh Pure Silk Qum Approx. 5' x 3'	1 500	5 000	12 000	18 000	10 000	33 000	79 920	133 200
PAPER MONEY — Compare the above with an investment of R10 000 at 10% interest per annum, compounded.					10 000	13 310	19 487	23 579

Source: Trigon Diamond Investment Group.
Carlton Centre, Johannesburg.

JOHANNESBURG STOCK EXCHANGE

Foreigners have the option of buying South African shares overseas or directly through the Johannesburg Stock Exchange. Many of South Africa's leading mining and industrial shares are traded, if not actually quoted, on European and North American stock exchanges. Prices are available in French, Belgian and Swiss francs, German marks, U.S. dollars and Sterling from banks and stockbrokers in these countries.

Buying shares

Although shares can be bought through banks and brokers in Europe and North America, there are still those who prefer to deal directly with the JSE through a Johannesburg stockbroker.

Before an account can be opened with a brokerage house in South Africa a client needs to have an introduction and/or bank reference. The rules of the JSE require that its membership "know their clients". While it is possible for foreign clients to deal with the JSE directly without a South African bank account, having one simplifies matters.

Financial rand

Regardless of whether transactions are done from overseas or by non-residents in South Africa itself, deals are in terms of Financial Rand. South Africa maintains a dual currency system — Financial Rand (FR) and Commercial Rand (CR). (See also FOREIGN EXCHANGE CONTROL).

Commercial Rand is used for normal trading and commercial transactions as well as payments of dividends from South Africa. The rate is determined by the South African Reserve Bank as the Central Bank in terms of U.S. dollars. In other words, the Reserve Bank sets the rate and the local commercial banks follow suit.

Financial Rand, on the other hand, is used primarily by foreigners for investment transactions in South Africa. The price of this currency is largely influenced by supply and demand and normally tends to be available at a much cheaper rate to the foreigner than Commercial Rand.

Dividends to foreign shareholders are paid in Commercial Rand and are freely transferable — after deduction of a maximum of fifteen percent non-resident shareholders tax (See TAXES and ESTABLISHING A COMPANY). The proceeds from sales of shares purchased with Financial Rand, however, are in FRs again and can be transferred overseas only in terms of the going rate for this currency.

In buying South African shares, the foreign investor therefore pays less than the going Rand price by utilising the discount available through Financial Rands. Past experience has shown that sometimes a dramatic increase in the FR rate alone can result in impressive profits for overseas buyers of S.A. shares. This makes it important for foreign investors to consider both the prices of the shares themselves and the FR rate when buying. Expectations are, incidentally, that ideally sometime in the future, the FR and CR rates will get closer and finally merge. In the meantime, however, the distinction remains.

ADRs

Foreign purchasers of South African shares can register them in their own name at their home address or else purchase title to these shares through the vehicle of American Depositary Receipts (ADRs) or receipts issued by EUROCLEAR, SICOVAM or SOGE (European nominee companies). For example, the American issuer of ADRs arranges for the shares to be lodged with a bank in South Africa which registers them in the name of a nominee company while a receipt (American Depositary Receipt) for the shares is being issued to the purchaser. These ADRs are freely negotiable. Thus foreign shareholders can acquire South African shares at a discount of around 35% at present, which means that their return is grossed up by some 50%.

Performance

There is considerable overseas interest in what happens on the South African stock market. Especially in gold shares, foreign investment is high. On a weighted average overseas investors hold 38,7 percent of all these shares, with American buyers in the forefront at an average of 23,2 percent of the overall total.

But performance in other sectors happened to be equally impressive lately. In 1979, for instance, the Johannesburg Stock Exchange was the best performing major stock market in the world. In that year fortunes could have been made in all but a handful of market sectors. Daily trading values accelerated from a January average of R5,5 million to a December average of over R12 million per day. As the eighties started the daily total rose to a daily average of around R20 million with a high of R43 million in September 1980.

Information

For those interested in obtaining detailed information about the JSE and the shares listed there are several publications available. The JSE annually publishes a two-volume Stock Exchange Handbook containing complete information about companies listed, as well as monthly bulletins with updated data. These can be obtained at reasonable prices by writing to:

Public Relations Department
Johannesburg Stock Exchange
P.O. Box 1174
Johannesburg 2000

Chapter 8

TROUBLE SPOTS

DISINVESTMENT PRESSURES

Investors in South Africa are bound to encounter the wrath of some pressure groups abroad who believe that dealing with that country is evil. Varying in size and impact, about a hundred such groups have made it their task to discourage new foreign investment in South Africa and to promote severance of all its existing financial links with the outside world.

Campaign

With the approval of especially the Third World and Communist countries in the United Nations, as well as organisations such as the International Labour Organisation and the World Council of Churches, these pressure groups have been waging a vigorous disinvestment campaign for more than ten years. Apart from appearances at church, university campus and community gatherings, these activist groups have kept the issue alive through films, pamphlets, news releases and the like.

To publicise their cause in the media, these pressure groups often organise debates and demonstrate in the street against selected targets such as banks, stores and business offices. Another method applied in especially Britain and the United States is to dramatise the disinvestment cause by way of resolutions before annual general meetings. In instances where the activists themselves cannot muster enough proxy votes, they have actually purchased shares to give them a voice at such meetings.

In 1980 American corporate involvement was the theme of at least 45 resolutions submitted at 38 separate annual general meetings in the United States — outnumbering any other single issue by far. Although all these resolutions were defeated, they served to gain wide publicity and some embarrassment for the corporations at which they were aimed. The intent is clear: To intimidate and harrass corporations to the point where they would desist from further involvement in South Africa for the sake of peace of mind.

These disinvestment activists insist that foreign investment buttresses apartheid — an "evil system designed to oppress blacks." They contend that economic isolation would topple the white South African government and bring an end to apartheid — making way for black majority rule. They concede that it may bring some hardship to black South Africa, but maintain that all this suffering will be for a worthwhile cause: freedom from oppression.

South Africans

On the other hand South Africans — both black and white, supporters of the government and opponents — have dismissed the disinvestment campaign as irresponsible, inconsistent, illogical and insensitive to the real needs of the people.

They point out:

★ That instead of propping up apartheid, foreign investment actually serves to break down barriers through economic integration.

★ That instead of helping the black man, such embargoes and disinvestment would lead to large-scale unemployment, hunger and despair, for especially the black worker.

★ That these pressure groups are using the blacks in South Africa as pawns to accomplish their own brand of government in that part of the world, which would be decidedly Marxist as opposed to the present pro-Western regime.

★ That the activists have never raised their voices or showed any opposition to business links with other "more deserving" targets, such as Russia, Vietnam and Cuba.

★ That these pressure groups have no mandate from South Africa's black peoples to speak and act on their behalf in trying to discourage investment and trade.

★ That the black peoples of South Africa are overwhelmingly in favour of increased investment from abroad as it brings prosperity and development to its ranks.

Debate

This debate is bound to continue. So are the efforts of the disinvestment forces, according to statements by its leaders. Thus far it has had very little real effect on the continued flow of investment from abroad. But, the protesters insist, as their campaign gains momentum they will succeed in curtailing this inflow of capital.

In the meantime, foreign corporations have found a way to respond effectively to the situation in South Africa. Through co-operation with less strident pressure groups — the Sullivan Committee, EEC and SACCOLA — business in South Africa has been making planned progress towards job and pay equality and the elimination of discrimination in general. (See LABOUR CODES and LABOUR PRACTICES).

LABOUR CODES

As disinvestment pressures built up against South Africa abroad, steps were taken by more moderate groups in and outside that country to improve the working conditions of the black worker. Some insist that these efforts came as a direct response to the more militant forces bent on isolating South Africa economically, while others disclaim any connection between the two. (See also DISINVESTMENT PRESSURES).

At least nine different so-called *employment codes* have been drawn up by these more moderate pressure groups to encourage greater corporate responsibility in the area of black labour in South Africa. Only three survived:

1. *The Sullivan Code:* This code was drawn up by Reverend Leon Sullivan for U.S. affiliated companies in South Africa. Compliance is voluntary and at the latest count about fifty percent of the three hundred and fifty American companies with operations in South Africa are signatories. These signatories of the Sullivan Code are required to report back annually on the progress made and are rated accordingly in one of the following three categories:

   (i) Making Good Progress.
   (ii) Making Acceptable Progress.
   (iii) Need To Become More Active.

   These U.S. affiliated firms are judged on the basis of their performance in the following respects:

   ★ Nonsegregation of races in all eating, comfort and work facilities.
   ★ Equal and fair employment practices for all races.
   ★ Equal pay for comparable work.
   ★ Training programmes to prepare blacks and other non-whites for supervisory, administrative, clerical, and technical jobs in substantial numbers.
   ★ More blacks and other non-whites in management and supervisory positions.
   ★ Improving employees' lives outside the work environment in such areas as housing, transportation, schooling, recreation and health.

2. *The EEC Code:* The EEC Code was drawn up by the nine governments of the European Economic Community for British and European subsidiary companies. The British government actually publishes an explanatory and detailed guide to the EEC Code, and requires that British parent companies with more than fifty percent holdings in South African operations report back annually. As in the case of the Sullivan Principles, the EEC Code urges European parent companies to improve the working conditions, wages, and fringe benefits of black workers at their South African subsidiaries.

125

3. *SACCOLA Code:* This is an indigenous Code drawn up by the Urban Foundation and SACCOLA for South African employers. The Urban Foundation is a private body striving for improvement of the quality of life of South Africa's black communities, while SACCOLA (the South African Employers Consultative Committee on Labour Affairs) represents commerce and industry in that country. Once again the SACCOLA Code expresses itself in favour of job and wage equality and equal working conditions for all races.

Measuring up

These codes are hardly revolutionary. Still there are some foreign companies who have steadfastly refused to be signed up in the belief that they constitute interference in their own business affairs. Signatories, however, maintain that improving the position of the black worker in an organised fashion, serves not only to stabilise their growing black work force, but to blunt the attacks of the militant disinvestment forces. Scoring well in terms of the Sullivan and EEC Codes does indeed help to strengthen the position of foreign companies when confronted by the militants; and with companies themselves involved in overseeing these codes, good scores go a long way towards peer approval and prestige.

Official attitude

When the Sullivan Code was first introduced in the mid-seventies, the South African government gave its approval — pointing out that the principles enunciated were very much in line with its own continued efforts to improve the position of the black worker. At the same time it expressed the hope that these principles would also apply in other parts of the world where America does business.

The South African government has been engaged in extensive programmes to promote equal opportunity and pay for all races. More recently the Wiehahn and Riekert Commissions have been appointed to streamline and improve labour practices. (See LABOUR PRACTICES). At the same time, the authorities in South Africa have displayed resentment towards any signs of undue interference in politics by business groups in or outside the country.

A good measure of South Africa's official sensitivity in this area is for instance the Protection of Businesses Act, which makes it illegal for any person or business to furnish details on order, direction or request from abroad without permission from the Minister of Industries, Commerce and Consumer Affairs. This wording is actually broad enough to even prohibit firms from reporting back to Sullivan or the EEC, but until now such permission has been granted without exception.

ARMS EMBARGO

In August 1963, the United Nations Security Council passed a non-binding resolution calling upon all its member states to prohibit the sales and shipment of arms to South Africa. This was advertised as an expression of the world's opposition to *apartheid* and ostensibly implemented to withhold the tools of oppression from the South African government. Although the United States, Canada and Britain applied this embargo, France continued to sell sophisticated equipment to South Africa — amounting to billions in trade. In November 1977, the U.N. Security Council attempted to close the loopholes by declaring the situation in South Africa a threat to world peace and making the arms embargo mandatory on all member states.

South Africa is not exactly shopping around these days for military hardware. Ever since the first mention of an arms boycott it actively worked towards self-sufficiency in the essential items. Today it is manufacturing under license French Mirage jets as well as its own modified version of the Italian Aermacchi fighter-trainer and an improved version of the French Panhard armoured car, known as the Eland. It has already indicated that withdrawal of these licenses would not deter it from continuing manufacturing these and other items. It has developed its own guided missiles and has become an exporter of arms.

In some countries, notably the United States, exporters should note that civilian items with possible military application may be on the administration's so-called grey area or dual purpose list — and subject to special approval before they can be sold to South Africa.

Chapter 9

VISITING

USEFUL TIPS

Monetary

The currency unit in South Africa is the Rand, denoted by the symbol R. One Rand equals 100 cents.

Coins in circulation: 1 Rand, 50 cents, 20 cents, 10 cents, 5 cents, 2 cents, 1 cent and ½ cent.

Banknotes: R20, R10, R5, R2 and R1.

Electricity

All power systems 220/230 volts except Pretoria (240 volts) and Port Elizabeth (220/250 volts) A.C. at 50 cycles per second.

Tap water

All tap water is safe and drinkable.

Clothing

Suits and ties are always worn for business, while casual dress may be in order at barbeques and at game reserves. Light and medium-weight suits are adequate for all seasons and in winter raincoats will suffice. (See CLIMATE).

Business hours

Normally Monday to Friday 0830 to 1700 hours with luncheon between 1300 and 1400.

Shopping hours

Monday to Friday 0830 to 1700 hours, Saturdays, 0830 to 1300 hours.

Banking hours

0900 until 1530 hours every weekday except Wednesday when banks close at 1300 hours. On Saturdays from 0800 until 1100 hours.

Tipping

Service charges are not added to restaurant bills and a tip of 10-15% is in order. Porters, room attendants etc. are accustomed to receiving up to 40 cents for small favours, while a normal one or two-bag load "entitles" porters to 50 cents.

CLIMATE

South Africa is situated in the southern hemisphere and as such has its summer from October to March and winter from April to September. Despite some drastic differences between regions, its climate can generally be described as temperate. South Africa, incidentally, never fails to remind prospective visitors that they are coming to the country with one of the highest sunshine ratings in the world. Cape Town, for example, enjoys 3 092 hours of sunshine per normal year. This in comparison with London (1 480 hours), Washington (2 200), Madrid (2 910), Rome (2 360) and Paris (1 740).

Rainfall in the interior is usually in summer and often comes in thunderstorms, while the Cape coastal area relies mostly on winter rains. Durban and surrounding areas are subtropical with high humidity in summer. Apart from white-capped peaks in the high mountains during midwinter, snow is still the exception.

The following temperatures are in degrees Celsius:

Coastal Cities	Average temp. Summer	Average temp. Winter	Average Sea temp.	Average sun-hours per day
Cape Town	21,5	13	21 (False Bay)	8,4
Durban	24	16,5	18,5-26,5	6,6
Port Elizabeth	21	13,5	17-23,5	7,9
East London	21,5	15,5	18,5-21	7,5
Inland Cities			Altitude (metres)	
Pretoria	22,5	11,5	1 370	8,9
Johannesburg	21	10,5	1 750	8,7
Bloemfontein	22,5	10,5	1 390	9,3
Kimberley	25	10,5	1 220	9,4

VISAS AND HEALTH REQUIREMENTS

Most foreigners are required to have visas to visit South Africa. Applications should be submitted on standard application forms to South African diplomatic missions abroad, together with passports.

In countries where South Africa does not have diplomatic representation, application can be made directly to the Secretary for the Interior, Pretoria. Applications can also be transmitted through an airline, shipping company or travel agency arranging the applicant's visit.

In cases of extreme urgency, where an applicant wishes to receive permission, by telegram or cable, to enter South Africa, he is required to pay a fee of R7.00. On arrival he will be required to show the telegram or cable to passport control which will then proceed to stamp a visa in his passport. An applicant who is not able to apply for a visa in person is required to attach two passport size photographs signed on the reverse side. With few exceptions, visas to nationals of all countries are free of charge.

Health requirements

Visitors are required to be in possession of an *International Health Certificate* with certification of a valid vaccination against *smallpox.*

Yellow fever vaccination is required in cases of all visitors who travelled through or stopped over at any place or port within what was formerly known as the yellow fever endemic zone of Africa — it lies roughly between the 15 and 10 parallels. Exempted are passengers on a scheduled flight in transit, providing that they remain within the precincts of airports within this area.

Cholera vaccination is necessary for all persons arriving in South Africa from Central or North African countries and from countries in Asia east of longitude 60 degrees E. Exempted from this requirement are passengers on scheduled flights in transit.

CUSTOMS REQUIREMENTS FOR VISITORS

Visitors to South Africa are entitled to bring with them duty-free the following:

★ Used personal effects and used sporting or recreational equipment.

★ One litre of alcoholic beverage;
  One litre of wine;
  400 cigarettes; 50 cigars;
  250 grams of cigarette or pipe tobacco;
  300ml. of perfume.
  Other items — new or used — to a total value not exceeding R80.

They are also allowed to carry with them South African banknotes not exceeding R100.

If visiting foreigners are within these limits, they need only on entry at any of South Africa's international ports or airports follow the green arrow denoting NOTHING TO DECLARE. There is, of course, still the chance that they may be asked by a customs officer to declare the goods in their possession.

Should they exceed any of these limits, visitors are obliged to use the GOODS TO DECLARE channel, indicated by a Red Arrow.

Also to be declared are any goods intended for commercial or trade purposes as well as samples.

Usually duty is levied at a rate of 20% of the value of the goods or items in question.

Everyone is prohibited from bringing into the country agricultural products such as meat, seeds, plants and bulbs, drugs or medicines, dangerous weapons, or obscene publications.

CAR TRAVEL

Visitors who intend to spend all their business and pleasure hours in the city centres of South Africa, can rely on public transport and taxicabs. Taxis are readily available around the major hotels. Between airports and major hotels special courtesy buses operate, apart from other regular scheduled bus services.

Car rental

Should a businessman, however, prefer to be independently mobile from the moment of arrival until he departs, he can rely on a number of car rental services. Most maintain offices at airports and in major cities and towns. They include the internationally renowned Avis and Hertz, as well as a few local ones.

Rental rates and special discounts vary and change frequently and the economy-minded are well advised to check around for the best rate. It may be necessary to make reservations well ahead especially during the South African holiday season.

Rule of road

From the moment a foreigner slides in behind the steering of his rent-a-car — it will be on the right side — he should start thinking left. This is no problem for visitors from the few remaining countries such as Britain, New Zealand and Australia, where the rule of the road is to keep to the left. But others should make a conscious effort at all times to think left unless they want to meet the oncoming traffic head on!

Other points worth remembering are the following:

★ Speed limits are very strictly enforced in South Africa in an effort to conserve fuel. Penalties are severe. The limit on open roads, unless otherwise indicated, is 90km per hour.

★ Both driver and front seat passenger are required to wear seat belts at all times. This regulation is strictly enforced.

★ A driver with an alcohol content of more than 0.08 percent per 100 millilitre of blood is liable to be prosecuted, if caught.

In case of an accident where damage or injury results, the driver should remain on the scene of the accident after rendering emergency assistance and calling the nearest police station. In accidents where no injuries are sustained and only minor damage resulting, the police may instruct the party or parties involved to proceed to the station and make a statement.

Foreign visitors are permitted to use their drivers' licences or internationally recognised driving permits.

Foreign executives who are accustomed to being chauffeur-driven can obtain such services in all the major cities. Some of these chauffeur-driven cars are also available for special excursions to scenic areas and game reserves.

HOTELS

Visitors need not resort to tour guides to obtain information about South African hotels. It is all made simple by the Hotel Board. Establishments are classified from one-star to five. Unless a visitor intends to seek solace in the rural quiet of South Africa, it is unlikely that he will ever encounter any hotel under a three-star rating.

The Hotel Board describes three-star hotels as "excellent", four-star as "outstanding" and five-star as "comparable to the best in the world."

Like road signs, hotel ratings have become a fixture on hotel fronts in South Africa. Those who wish to display one-upmanship on their South African hosts who generally have no clue of what it all means, need only remember the following: This insignia on graded hotels — it is displayed both at entrances and rather proudly on letterheads of establishments — indicates: A five-star rating; more than half of its occupance is transitory (T); and it is licensed to sell wines, spirits, and beer (YYY).

YY would indicate that a hotel is licensed to sell only wines and beer — and Y, that a hotel is licensed only to sell wines and beer *during* meals. A dash (—) means exactly what it is supposed to stand for: nothing not even at meals. A dry hotel. T/R would indicate that 25 to 50% of the hotel's occupancy is transient and R that more than 75% of the residents are resident.

Try this insignia game on your host, but don't ask him whether the water is safe at any hotel anywhere in South Africa. He will be offended. The water *is* safe. It is Africa, but it is safe all the same.

Following is a list of hotels, three-star and above, in the major centres in South Africa.

Johannesburg

LANDDROST HOTEL *****
Plein Street
P.O. Box 11026
Johannesburg
Tel: 28 1770
Telex: 8-4092 SA

ROSEBANK HOTEL****
Turwhitt & Sturdee Ave.
P.O. Box 52025
Saxonwold
Tel: 788 1820

CARLTON HOTEL*****
Main Street
PO. Box 7709
Johannesburg
Tel: 21 8911
Telex: 8-6130 SA

SUNNYSIDE PARK
HOTEL***
2 York Road
P.O. Box 31256
Braamfontein
Tel: 643 3011
Telex: 8-7193 SA

TOWERS HOTEL****
Church Street
P.O. Box 535
Johannesburg
Tel: 836 7911
Telex: 8-0349 SA

PRESIDENT HOTEL
HOLIDAY INN***
Eloff & Plein Sts.
P.O. Box 7702
Johannesburg
Tel: 28 1414
Telex: 8-0448 SA

RAND INTERNATIONAL
HOTEL****
290 Bree Street
P.O. Box 4235
Johannesburg
Tel: 836 7911

**Jan Smuts Airport
Johannesburg**

SOUTHERN SUN
AIRPORT HOTEL***
Hulley Rd. Isando
Private Bag 6
Jan Smuts Airport
Tel: 36 2687/36 6911
Telex: 8-4870 SA

HOLIDAY INN***
Jan Smuts Airport
P.O. Box 388
Kempton Park
Tel: 975 1121
Telex: 8-6313 SA

Durban

MAHARANI HOTEL*****
Snell Parade
Durban
Tel: 32 7361
Telex: 6-2485

ROYAL HOTEL****
267 Smith Street
Durban
Tel: 32 0331

ELANGENI HOTEL****
Snell Parade
Durban
Tel: 37 1321
Telex: 60133

EDWARD HOTEL****
Jarine Parade
Durban
Tel: 37 3681

Cape Town

PRESIDENT HOTEL*****
Beach Road,
P.O. Box 62
Sea Point, Cape Town
Tel: 41 1121
Telex: 57-7973SA

MOUNT NELSON
HOTEL*****
Orange Street
P.O. Box 2608
Cape Town
Tel: 22 0012
57-7804SA

HEERENGRACHT
HOTEL*****
St. George's Street
P.O. Box 2936
Cape Town
Tel: 41 3151
Telex: 57-0031 SA

De WAAL HOTEL****
Mill Street
P.O. Box 2793
Gardens, Cape Town
Tel: 45 1311
Telex: 57-0653 SA

NEWLANDS HOTEL****
Main Road
Newlands, Cape Town
Tel: 65 4180
Telex: 57-0686 SA

ARTHUR'S SEAT
HOTEL***
Arthur's Road
Sea Point, Cape Town
Tel: 44 3344

Pretoria

BURGERSPARK HOTEL****
Cnr. Minnaar and
Van der Walt Sts.
P.O. Box 2301 Pretoria
Tel: 28 6570
Telex: 30325 SA

BOULEVARD HOTEL***
186 Struben Street
Pretoria
Tel: 26 4806
Telex: 3-752 SA

Bloemfontein

THE BLOEMFONTEIN****
East Burger Street
P.O. Box 2212
Bloemfontein
Tel: 7 0595
Telex: 27039

PRESIDENT HOTEL***
1 Union Avenue
P.O. Box 1851
Bloemfontein
Tel: 7 0666

Port Elizabeth

ELIZABETH HOTEL*****
La Roche Drive
P.O. Box 13100
Port Elizabeth
Tel: 52 3720
Telex: 74 7498 SA

BEACH HOTEL***
Marine Drive
Port Elizabeth
Tel: 53 2161
Telex: 74-7642 SA

MARINE HOTEL***
Marine Drive
P.O. Box 501
Port Elizabeth
Tel: 53 2101
Telex: 74-7515 SA

East London

CARLTON HOTEL***
25 Inverleith Terrace
P.O. Box 178
East London
Tel: 2 3174

KENNAWAY HOTEL***
Esplanade
P.O. Box 583
East London
Tel: 2 5531

KINGS HOTEL***
Esplanade
P.O. Box 587
East London
Tel: 2 2561

RESTAURANTS

A business deal often starts with a meal. In this respect South Africa is no exception. Business luncheons (and to a large extent, dinners) are very much part of the commercial community.

Foreign visitors who wish to entertain close to where they are staying will have no problem in finding adequate to excellent eating places in any of the major hotels. For those who wish to broaden their experience — and perhaps their waistline — there is also an interesting array of independent eating establishments to choose from.

French, Italian and Greek as well as other internationally recognised European foods are served at reasonable prices. In South Africa, according to culinary experts, good food is still bought cheaply in comparison with other developed parts of the world.

Local food

But what about the adventurous visitor who wants to get a taste of the local in food? His first problem is to determine what is meant by local. The early Dutch, German, French, Malay, English, and Indian settlers all contributed in one way or another to the local food scene.

In Cape Town the visitor may find his way by asking for *Kaapse kos* (Cape food) and in Johannesburg he may end up eating about the same dishes by insisting on *boerekos* (farmer's food). In especially the Cape dishes — but also in other parts of the country where traditional foods are served — the visitor should prepare for a strong strain of Malay influence. *Bredie* (mutton and vegetable mix), *atjar* (pickles), curried meat and fish, and *bobotie* (spiced minced meat dish) are some examples. *Koeksisters* and *melktert* (milk tart) are some of the farmer's specialities in desserts and *biltong* (dried meat in sliced form) is devoured before, during and after meals.

Anyone who wishes to eat Indian curry until his mouth and eyes water will have to wait until he gets to Durban. Other cities have substitutes but the real thing is basically to be found in this city where there is the largest concentration of Indians.

Local wines and cheese of good quality are available at prices considerably lower than those of comparable imports.

The following list of restaurants is not in order of preference or rating. It is merely a short guide to good dining in cities likely to be visited by foreign executives:

137

Johannesburg

BARNATO'S
Landdrost Hotel
Plein Street
Tel: 28 1770

Continental menu, specialising in beef.

POT LUCK
Melle and Smit Sts.
Tel: 725 5543

French menu

L'ESCARGOT
85 Fourth Avenue
Melville
Tel: 726 5411

Continental cuisine in converted old house. Unlicensed — bring own wine.

FREDDIES PARKMORE TAVERN
11th Avenue, Parkmore
Sandton
Tel: 783 1500

Continental cuisine in converted old house. Unlicensed — bring own wine.

Le FRANCAIS
The Mall
Rosebank
Tel: 788 8400

French cuisine

THREE SHIPS
Carlton Hotel
Main Street
Tel: 21 8911

Continental Cuisine

FISHERMANS GROTTO
14a Plein Street
Johannesburg
Tel: 834 7000

Seafood

CHEZ ANDRE
49 Kruis Street
Johannesburg
Tel: 23 3662

French menu

CHEZ MARIANO
Kine Center
Commissioner Street
Johannesburg
Tel: 21 8441

French — Italian

Dinner/Dancing

ANNABEL'S
Landdrost Hotel
Plein Street
Tel: 28 1770

Cabaret, dancing. Continental menu.

RAFFLES
Rand International Hotel
Bree Street
Tel: 836 7911

Disco dancing, dining

Pretoria

AMBASSADEUR
Burgerspark Hotel
Van der Walt St.
Tel: 48 6570

Continental. Specialising in seafoods.

HOF VAN HOLLAND
Lynnwood Road Ext.
Tel: 87 1112
Dutch decor and Indonesian dishes including Rijstafel.

THE LOMBARDY
Lynnwood Road Ext.
Tel: 87 1284
Italian-French Restaurant in converted farmhouse.

LA BOHEME
Volkskas Building
Pretorius Street
Tel: 41 1676
Top of Pretoria's highest building. Continental.

FLAMINGO ROOM
Hotel Boulevard
186 Struben Street
Tel: 2 4806
Continental with some local dishes.

Cape Town:

CAPE KITCHEN
Heerengracht Hotel
Trust Bank Centre
Tel: 41 3151
Continental food, specialising in seafood.

GRILL ROOM
Mount Nelson Hotel
Orange Street
Tel: 22 0012
Continental food in Edwardian type decor.

KAAPSE TAFEL
90 Queen Victoria St.
Tel: 22 0489
Traditional and local dishes. Unlicensed.

BELLINZONA RESTAURANT
1 Beach Road
Table View
Tel: 57 3011
French cuisine with seafoods. Unlicensed.

ONS HUISIE
Bloubergstrand
Tel: 56 1553
Traditional and seafood in thatched fisherman's cottage.

ROUND HOUSE
The Glen
Camps Bay
Tel: 48 7193
Continental food in historic setting.

Dinner/Dancing

RAFFLES
President Hotel
Seapoint
Tel: 44 1121
Disco & Supper Club

VAN DONCK
Heerengracht Hotel
Trust Bank Centre
Tel: 41 3151
Continental food. Dancing

MAXIMS
27 Wale Street
Cape Town
Tel: 22 8145
Private Club, "Daily Membership" available for visitors. Continental food. Dancing.

Stellenbosch

Many visitors drive fifty kilometres from Cape Town to this historical university village. Not only to see the sights, but to eat at one of several pleasant restaurants in restored seventeenth-century estate houses. These are some notable examples:

LANZERAC
Jonkershoek Road
Stellenbosch
Tel: (02231) 7 1132
Traditional Cape dishes. Old wine estate.

VOLKSKOMBUIS
Old Strand Road
Stellenbosch
Tel: (02231) 7 2121
Traditional Cape dishes. In restored old residence.

DE KELDER
63 Dorp Street
Stellenbosch
Tel: (02231) 3797
Continental and traditional. In restored old residence.

Durban

CRYSTAL ROOM
Maharani Hotel
Tel: 32 7361
French cuisine

PAPADUM
Maharani Hotel
Tel: 32 7361
Curries — buffet style.

SALTORI'S
320 West Street
Tel: 32 9558
Continental food.

OLD ROMA
193 Smith Street
Tel: 37 3872
International with emphasis on Italian dishes.

LE BEAUJOLAIS
John Milne Road
Tel: 37 7066
French bistro style

THE 67 RESTAURANT
16 Albany Grove
Tel: (63367) 32 3838
Italian dishes.

THE QUEEN'S TAVERN
16 Stamford Hill Road
Tel: 6 1846
Indian and Middle Eastern dishes.

Dinner/Dancing

RAFFLES
Maharani Hotel
Tel: 32 7361
Supper club on 31st floor. Continental food & dancing.

COPACABANA
Beverley Hills Hotel
Umhlanga Rocks
Tel: 51 2211
Continental food. Dancing.

ROMA RESTAURANT
193 Smith Street
Tel: 37 3872
International dishes. Dancing.

East London

CAPTAINS TABLE
Holiday Inn
Marina Glen
Tel: 2 7260

Swiss cuisine

MOVENPICK
Orient Pavilion
Beach Front
Tel: 2 1840

Continental food. Dancing some nights.

TALK OF THE TOWN
Inverleith Terrace
Tel: 2 3174

Continental food.

Dinner/Dancing

THE COLETTE
Hotel Kennaway
Beach Front
Tel: 2 5531

Continental food. Dancing.

Port Elizabeth

ROOM AT THE TOP
Hotel Elizabeth
Humewood
Tel: 52 3720

Continental food. Dancing at night.

SIR RUFANE DONKIN ROOMS
Upper Hill Street
Tel: 2 5534

Historic home transferred into restaurant. Table d'hote/unlicensed.

THE CORNFLOWER
Constantia Centre North
Tel: 54 1315

German and seafood.

LOS CHICOS
Clarendon Hotel
Lutman St.
Tel: 2 1558

Spanish specialising in seafood.

USEFUL DIPLOMATIC ADDRESSES

South African Representatives abroad and address:

Representatives of Foreign Country in South Africa and address:

Argentina

Ambassador E & P
Avenida Marcelo t de Alvear
590/8⁰ Piso
BUENO AIRES
Tel. Add: "SALEG"
Tel. 31 8991/7
Telex: 122095

Chargé d' Affaires
1059 Church Street
Hatfield
Pretoria 0002
Tel. 74 5957/78
Tel. Add: "EMBARGENTINA"

Australia

Ambassador E & P
Rhodes Place
Yarralumla
CANBERRA ACT 2600
Tel. Add: "SAKOM"
Tel. 73 2424/5/6/7 or 73 3912
Telex: 62734

Ambassador E & P
302 Standard Bank Chambers
Church Square
Pretoria 0002
Tel. 3 7051/2
Tel. Add: "AUSTEMBA"

Austria

Ambassador E & P
Renngasse 10/1
VIENNA A-1010
Tel. Add: "SALEG"
Tel. 63 06 56
Telex: 766 71 SALEG

Ambassador E & P
10th Floor Apollo Centre
405 Church St. East
(Cnr. Du Toit St.)
Pretoria 0002
Tel. 3 1020, 3 3001 and 3 0032
Tel. Add: "AUSTROAMB"

Belgium

Ambassador E & P
P.O. Box 7/8
Rue de la Loi 26
BRUSSELS 1040
Tel. Add: "LEGSA"
Tel. 230 6845
Telex: 21 381

Ambassador E & P
Muckleneuk
275 Pomona Street
Muckleneuk
Pretoria 0002
Tel. 44 3201
Telex: 30500 SA
Tel. Add: "AMBABEL"

Bolivia

Ambassador E & P
Avenida 6 de Agosto 2860
LA PAZ
Tel. Add: "SALEG"
Telex: SALEG BX5424
Tel. 6 4532, 2 3951

Charge d'Affaires en Titre
P.O. Box 27991
Sunnyside
Tel. 47 3797

Brazil

Ambassador E & P
Avenida dos Naqoes
LOTE 6
Caixa Postal 11-1170
70000 BRASILIA D F
Tel. Add: "SAREP"
Tel. 223 4873 223 1243 223 8087
223 8189

Chargé d'Affaires
1st Floor
African Eagle Life Centre
Cnr. Andries and
Vermeulen Streets
Pretoria 0002
Tel. 48 7018/9
Telex: 3 674
Tel. Add: "BRASEMB"

Canada

Ambassador E & P
15 Sussex Drive
OTTAWA KIM 1MB
Tel. Add: "SAKOM"
Tel. 749 5977

Ambassador E & P
Nedbank Plaza
Cnr. Church and Beatrix Streets
P.O. Box 26006 Arcadia
Tel. Add: "CANDOM"
Tel. 48 7062

Chile

Ambassador E & P
Avenida Pedro de Valdivia 800
Casilla 16189
SANTIAGO 9
Telex: 3520075 SALEG
Tel. Add: "SALEG"
Tel. 23 2319

Hon. Consul
1931 Sanlam Centre
Foreshore
P.O. Box 4063
Cape Town 8000
Tel. 47 1490
Telex: 57 7299

China (republic of)

Ambassador E & P
Sixth floor
Enterprise Building
54 Chungshen Road N Sec. 3
P.O. Box 540
TAIPEI TAIWAN
Tel. Add: "SALEG"
Tel. 596 8013/4
Telex: 21954 "SALEG"

Ambassador E & P
11th Floor
Old Mutual Centre
167 Andries Street
P.O. Box 649
Pretoria
Tel. 48 2034/5/6

Denmark

Consul-General
1st Floor Moentergade 1
DK-1011 COPENHAGEN K
Tel. (01) 14 6644
Tel. Add: "SAKONGEN"

Consul-General
Suite 2907
Carlton Centre
Commissioner Street
Johannesburg 2001
Tel. 21 6052
Tel. Add: "DONNEBROO"

Finland

Minister
Kapteeninkafu 11B 15
00140 HELSINKI 14
Tel. Add: "LEGSA"
Tel. 65 82 88

Chargé d'Affaires
171 Esselen Street
Sunnyside
Pretoria 0002
Tel. 44 2159 and 44 5211
Tel. Add: "FINLANDIA"

France

Ambassador E & P
59 Quai D'Orsay
PARIS 75007
Tel. Add: "SALEG"
Tel. 555 9237
Telex: 200280

Ambassador E & P
807 George Avenue
Arcadia
Pretoria 0002
Tel. 74 5564/5
Telex: 3 637
Tel. Add: "AMBAFRANCE"

Germany (Federal Republic)

Ambassador E & P
5300 Bonn-Bad Godesberg
3 Auf der Hostert
Tel. Add: "SALEG-BONN-BAD
GODESBERG"
Tel. (02221) 35 1091
Telex: 88 5720

Ambassador E & P
P.O. Box 2023
180 Blackwood Street
Arcadia
Pretoria 0002
Tel. 74 5931/2/3
Telex: 3696 SA
Tel. Add: "DIPLOGERMA
PRETORIA"

Greece

Ambassador E & P
Leoforos Vassilissis Sofias 69
ATHENS 140
Tel. Add: "SALEG"
Tel. 72 9050 or 72 9724

Ambassador E & P
995 Pretorius Street
Pretoria 0002
Tel. 74 7351/2
Tel. Add: "GREEK EMBASSY"

Hong Kong

Consul-General
701 AIA Building
1 Stubbs Road
HONG KONG
Tel. Add: "SATRACOM"
Tel. 574 3351/2
Telex: 83742

Israel

Ambassador E & P
P.O. Box 7138
TEL AVIV 64734
Tel. Add: "SACONSUL"
Tel. (03) 25 6147
Telex: (03) 34 1355

Ambassador E & P
9th Floor
Apollo Centre
405 Church Street
(Cnr. du Toit Street)
Pretoria 0002
Tel. 2 9008/9
Telex: 3 775 PR
Tel. Add: "MEMISRAEL
PRETORIA"

Italy

Ambassador E & P
Philips Building
Piazza Monte Grappa 4
ROME 00195
Tel. Add: "SALEG"
Tel. 360 8441
Telex: 62221 SALEGROM

Ambassador E & P
796 George Avenue
Arcadia
Pretoria 0002
Tel. 74 5541/2/3/4
Tel. Add: "ITALDIPL"

Japan

Consul-General
414 Zenkyoren Building
7-9 Hirakawa-cho-2-chome
Chiyoda-ku
TOKYO 102
Telex: SA Konsul J26208
Tel. 265 3366/7/8/9
Tel. Add: "SUIDAFRIKAANS"

Consul-General
First Floor
Prudential Assurance Building
28 Church Square
Pretoria 0002
Tel. 48 6733/4/5
Tel. Add: "RYOJI PRETORIA"

Malawi

Ambassador E & P
Mpico Building
City Centre
P.O. Box 30043
LILONGWE 3
Telex: 4255
Tel. Add: "SALEG" LL
Tel. 30888

Ambassador E & P
First Floor Delta Building
471 Monica Road
Lynnwood
Pretoria 0002
Tel. 47 1373/5/9
Tel. Add: "MALAWIAN"

Netherlands

Ambassador E & P
Wassenaarseweg 40
THE HAGUE
Tel. Add: "SALEG"
Tel. 92 4501/3/4
Telex: 33610

Ambassador E & P
First Floor Nedbank Building
Cnr. Church and Andries Sts.
Pretoria 0002
Tel. 3 6451/6
Telex: 3648
Tel. Add: "HOLLANDIA"

New Zealand

Consul-General
Federation House
95-99 Molesworth Street
P.O. Box 12045
WELLINGTON
Tel. Add: "SALEG"
Tel. 737 413/4
Telex: SALEG NZ 31068

Norway

Honorary Consul-General
Meltzersgaten 4
P.O. Box 2540
OSLO 2
Tel. 56 6570

Consul-General
1400 African Eagle Centre
2 St. George's Street
Cape Town 8001
Tel. 22 5177
Telex: 57 7678
Tel. Add: "NORKONS"

Paraguay

Ambassador E & P
4th Floor Banco Paraguayo
de Comercio
"SUDAMERIS" 4^0
Ind. Nacional Esq.
Cerro Cora
Casilla de Correo 1832
ASUNCION
Tel. Add: "SAFEM"
Tel. 44331/2
Telex: 917 PY ANTELCO B

Ambassador E & P
189 Strelizie Road
Waterkloof Heights
Pretoria 0002
Tel. 45 1081/2
Telex: 30338
Tel. Add: "EMBAPAR"

Peru

Consul-General
Edificio el Pacifico Washington
4^0 Piso
Natalio Sanchez 125
Plaza Washington
LIMA
Tel. Add: "SALEG"
Telex: 25675 PU
Tel. 24 7949

Honorary Consul-General
803 African Eagle Centre
2 St. George's Street
Cape Town 8001
Tel. 43 0991
Telex: 57 0524 SA
Tel. Add: "CONPER"

Portugal

Ambassador E & P
Avenida Luis Bivar 10
LISBON 1
Tel. Add: "SALEG"
Telex: 12894 P
Tel. 57 5246 or 53 5713

Ambassador E & P
261 Devenish Street
Muckleneuk
Pretoria 0002
Tel. 44 1914 and 44 5052

Spain

Ambassador E & P
Edificio Lista
Calle de Claudio Coello $91-7^0$
(Cnr. Ortega y Gasset)
MADRID 6
Tel. Add: "SALEG"
Tel. 225 3830/8/9
Telex: 44049 SAAME

Ambassador E & P
First Floor
African Eagle Life Centre
Cnr. Andries & Vermeulen Sts.
Pretoria 0002
Tel. 3 2777/8

Sweden

Minister
Linnègatan 76
11523 STOCKHOLM
Tel. Add: "LEGSA"
Tel. 24 3950/1/2/3/4
Telex: 12142 LEGSA S

Envoy Extraordinary &
Minister Plenipotentiary
The Old Mutual Centre
9th Floor
167 Andries Street
Pretoria 0002
Tel. 41 1050/41 1060
Tel. Add: "SVENSK"

Switzerland

Ambassador E & P
1 Jungfraustrasse
BERNE
Tel. Add: "SALEG"
Tel. 44 2011
Telex: 33852 SALEG CH

Ambassador E & P
818 George Avenue
Arcadia
Pretoria 0002
Tel. 74 7788/9
Telex: SA 3 716

Great Britain

Ambassador E & P
South Africa House
Trafalgar Square
LONDON WC 2 N 5DP
Tel. Add: "OPPOSITELY"
Telex: 26 7672
Tel. 01 930 4488

Ambassador E & P
"Greystoke"
6 Hill Street
Pretoria 0002
Tel. 74 3121
Tel. Add: "PRODROME"

United States of America

Ambassador E & P
3051 Massachusetts
Avenue NW
WASHINGTON DC 20008
Tel. Add: "SALEG"
Tel. (Area 202) 232 4400
Telex: 440300

Ambassador E & P
7th Floor
Thibault House
Pretorius Street
Pretoria 0002
Tel. 48 4266
Tel. Add: "AMEMBASSY"

Uruguay

Ambassador E & P
Edificio Artigas Rincon 487-2⁰
Casilla de Correo 498
MONTEVIDEO
Tel. Add: "SAFEM"
Tel. 98 6956 and 8 3634
Telex: 393 SAFEM UY

Chargé d'Affaires
105 BP Centre
Cape Town
8001
Tel. 41 1581
Tel. Add: "URUSUD"

WEEKENDS

Chances are that those on short business trips may face a weekend in Johannesburg. It is an experience to avoid, unless there is a host in Johannesburg who insists that the visitor be his guest — or the traveller wishes to catch up on lost sleep in his hotel room.

Even those who are partial to the "golden city" during bustling weekdays, turn off and away over weekends. From Saturday afternoons at 1 p.m. when the stores close, until Monday morning a stillness descends over empty office buildings and yellow mine dumps surrounding them. There are of course parks, a zoo, and charming restaurants as well as theatre and cinema on Saturday. On Sunday even the theatres and cinemas close up.

For those who did not manage to rearrange their itineraries to allow for weekends at beach resort cities such as Cape Town or Durban, there are alternative escape routes.

Several special tour operators and airline charter companies shuttle visitors to game reserves some four hundred and fifty kilometres northeast from Johannesburg. Leaving Saturday mornings and returning late Sunday afternoons, visitors are shown a full range of African wildlife at close range, while staying overnight in safari-type but quite comfortable and — in the case of some private reserves — luxurious accommodation.

An even more popular weekend escape from Johannesburg is Sun City, a luxurious resort, an easy drive, and only one-half hour's flying from Johannesburg. Fully equipped with a Gary Player designed golf course, a game park, tennis courts, and other recreational facilities, Sun City also offers gambling and stage extravaganzas comparable to the best of Las Vegas. The hotel — situated in the independent black state of Bophuthatswana — runs its own road and air shuttle from Johannesburg. Arrangements can be made after arrival in Johannesburg or through a travel agent before departure for South Africa. Early booking may be advisable in view of a growing number of visiting business executives who use this convenient weekend escape from Johannesburg.

As beach resorts, Cape Town, Durban, Port Elizabeth and East London all offer scenic weekend relaxation. In Cape Town visitors have the option of renting a car or a limousine service for a tour around the Cape Peninsula, considered by many as the fairest Cape of them all.

SHOPPING

Shopping in South Africa is not very different from Western Europe, North America, Japan and other developed parts of the world. The range of products and prices are about the same as far as durables are concerned, while essential non-durables tend to be somewhat cheaper.

Fashions in Europe and the United States have a strong influence on what people wear. Male clothing of a very good quality is sold at prices well below those abroad. In fact, it has become practice for some foreign business executives to buy clothes on working trips to South Africa.

In buying gifts, the visitor has a whole range of interesting choices:

Gold and diamonds: No bargain basement prices even in the world's major producing country, but local jewellery is of a fine quality.

Semi-precious stones: Available at reasonable prices are stones such as amethyst, rose quartz, topaz, verdite, melachite, and Transvaal jade.

Animal skins and Curios: Lion, leopard, elephant, zebra, crocodile and even ostrich skins find their way into conveniently situated stores as display items, handbags, briefcases and wallets. Also African carvings, and bead work, warthog teeth, ostrich eggs and ivory carvings feature in most curio stores.

Sculptures and paintings: Works by renowned South African artists — both black and white — are available at any of a number of art galleries in the major cities.

Wines: Local wines make good gifts. KWV has devised a method to make it easy for visiting foreigners by offering gift packs to be delivered in several countries overseas.

SPORT AND RECREATION

South Africa is a sportsman's country. Spectators in winter have a choice between rugby and soccer and in summer it is mostly cricket. Sun City, near Johannesburg, often provides the venue for world title boxing and other major sporting events. Kyalami is the site for one of the regular Grand Prix racing events.

Visitors who prefer to participate instead of being mere spectators, have an almost limitless choice. Clubs in South Africa, ranging from tennis to squash, and bowls to golf, are all anxious to receive foreign guests.

Following are a few pointers for active visiting executives:

Hunting

In a country which happens to be among the world's foremost wildlife conservationists, hunting is strictly and ecologically controlled. Season is from May to September. Several local agencies provide facilities. Permits for firearms carried by visitors are issued by customs officials at point of entry.

Angling

Surf and rock fishing around South Africa's coastline is unrestricted and outstanding. At several resorts visitors can also rely on specially equipped craft for deep-sea or off-shore fishing. The best rock and surf fishing is from November to April, while big-game fishing can be enjoyed year-round.

Golf

South Africa is not only the land of Gary Player and Bobby Locke, but also of spectacular golf courses. Most country clubs welcome visitors from abroad, although in some cases introductions are needed. Here are some of the notable courses: *Johannesburg* — Wanderers C.C., Johannesburg C.C. *Pretoria* — Pretoria Country Club, Zwartkops C.C. *Cape Town* — Mowbray G.C. Rondebosch G.C. *Durban* — Durban Country Club, Royal Durban C.C. At *Sun City* a course designed by Gary Player awaits visitors.

Squash and tennis

In all major centres in South Africa visitors have easy access to courts. Concierges at hotels are able to assist in this respect.

Horse racing

Visiting punters have no need to spend their time in hotel rooms over the weekend. Every major city has facilities — Johannesburg (Turffontein), Cape Town (Kenilworth) and Durban (Greyville).

SOUTH AFRICA

Distance Table
(in kms.)

	Bloemfontein	Bulawayo	Cape Town	Durban	East London	George	Johannesburg	Kimberley	L.M. (Maputo)	Pietermaritzburg	Port Elizabeth	Pretoria	Salisbury	Welkom
Windhoek	1562	2608	1489	2213	1900	1746	1770	1382	2372	2133	1806	1811	2867	1599
Welkom	152	1123	1177	619	696	912	270	263	819	539	829	326	1382	
Salisbury	1524	439	2549	1640	2068	2307	1112	1595	1302	1560	2201	1056		
Pretoria	468	979	1493	656	1012	1251	56	539	567	576	1145			
Port Elizabeth	677	1942	779	904	301	334	1089	726	1513	851				
Pietermaritzburg	571	1301	975	80	686	602	520	751	663					
L.M. (Maputo)	882	1043	1917	609	1265	1665	602	1063						
Kimberley	412	853	1437	600	956	733	483							
Johannesburg						1195								
George	760	2048	445	1239	630									
East London	544	1809	1080	656										
Durban	651	1381	1633											
Cape Town	1025	2290												
Bulawayo	1265													

AVIS

SOUTH AFRICA

Scale 1:10 500 000

| | | Railways

0 50 100 150 200 250 Kilometres

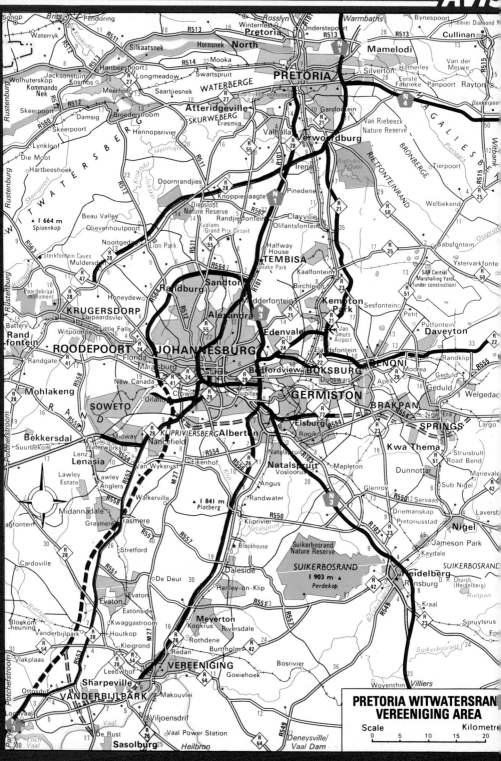

PRETORIA WITWATERSRAND
VEREENIGING AREA

Scale   Kilometre
0   5   10   15   20

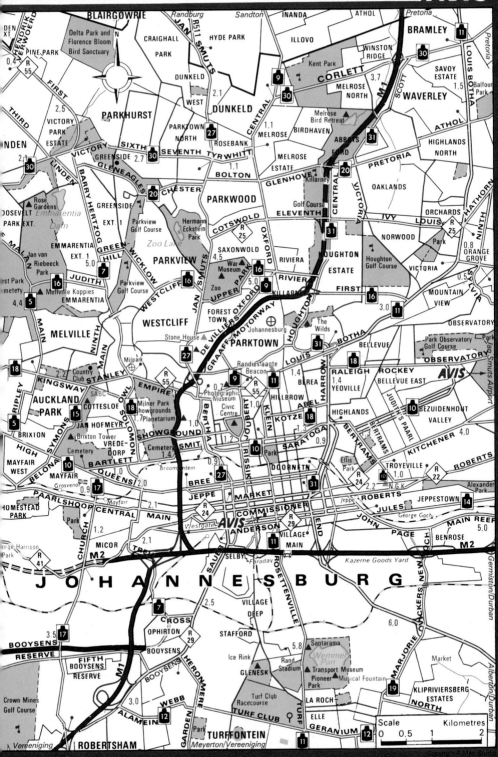

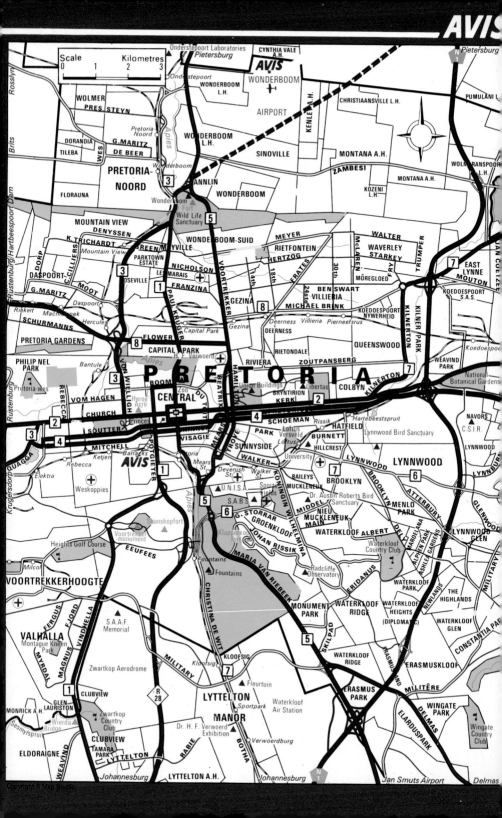

AVIS

CAPE PENINSULA

Scale — Kilometres
0 2 4 6 8

Copyright © Map Studio

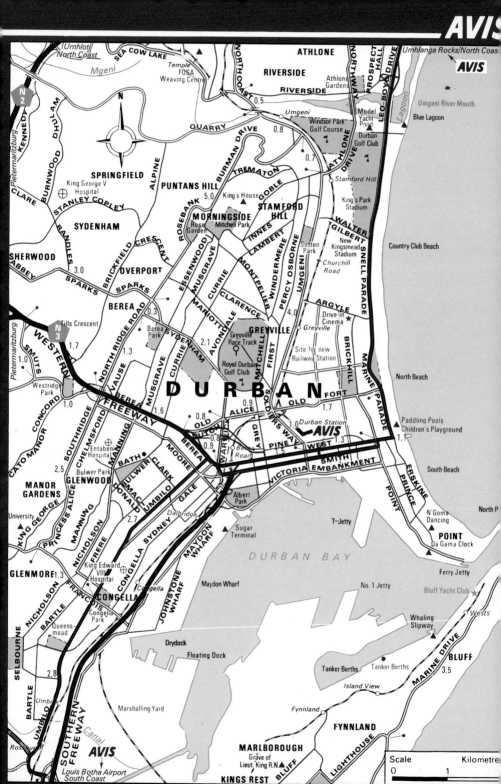